OUT OF PLACE IN AMERICA

OTHER BOOKS BY PETER SCHRAG

Village School Downtown

Voices in the Classroom

PETER SCHRAG

OUT OF PLACE IN AMERICA

Essays for the End of an Age

RANDOM HOUSE
New York

ISBN: 0–394–46004–9
Library of Congress Catalog Card Number:
74–140726
Some of these articles first appeared in
Harper's, Commentary, and the
Saturday Review.

Manufactured in the United States of America
by Haddon Craftsmen, Inc., Scranton, Pa.

9 8 7 6 5 4 3 2

First Edition

CONTENTS

Preface   vii

Out of Place in America:
  Confessions of a Chauvinist   3
The Forgotten American   14
Growing Up on Mechanic Street   35
What Happened to Main Street?   52
Tennessee's Lonesome End   74
White Man in Harlem   97
Erie: Life on a Dying Lake   110
Appalachia: Again the Forgotten Land   125
The Four-Year Generation   141
From Chicago to November   155
Why Our Schools Have Failed   169
The Secret Roots of Black Culture   191
The Romantic Critics of Education   208
The Schoolmasters   223
The End of the Great Tradition   237

For Diane

PREFACE

Most of these essays were written as magazine pieces between 1967 and 1970; each of them is concerned with life in America, and each was intended to be, in its own way, a discussion of the cultural news. It was not until I began to think of them as a group that I realized that each was an elaboration of a common theme, the theme of the first essay, "Out of Place in America." I have made very few revisions, although hindsight always makes such revisions tempting. "Out of Place in America" was written for this book, not in order to correct errors, but primarily as a mental profile of which each essay is a particular.

P. S.

OUT OF PLACE IN AMERICA

OUT OF PLACE IN AMERICA: CONFESSIONS OF A CHAUVINIST

On May 10, 1940, after eight months of what some people then called the phony war, the German Army and Air Force attacked the Netherlands, Belgium, and Luxembourg, thereby beginning the military rout which led, in a few weeks, to the fall of France and the occupation of most of Western Europe. We—my parents, my grandmother and I—were living in Brussels then, had been living there ever since the fall of 1939 when the Germans and Russians invaded Poland and the phony war began in the West: German Jewish refugees by way of Luxembourg, refugees of illusion who relied on Belgian neutrality and the willingness of Hitler to honor it. I knew little of those things then—no, knew nothing, except that as a boy of nine going to school in a Brussels suburb I had begun to call myself a Belgian.

The ensuing year constituted one of those common European adventures of wartime flight and survival—an abortive attempt to escape the German armies which led as far as Boulogne on the French coast, a forced return to Brussels and, ultimately, a successful escape—forged papers, professional (and amateur) smugglers, a cooperative railroad engineer who stopped a train just ahead of a Nazi control post, midnight walks across guarded frontiers, the fear of Gestapo calls in the night which never came, and, in the spring of 1941, the ship from Lisbon to New York. But what lingers most, after thirty years, is the response of that boy of nine—not quite nine—to the events of May 10. I remember thinking as the bombs fell on Brussels that sunny Tuesday morning that a world was coming to an end, that things would never be the same again. It seems a strangely precocious thought for a small person whose horizons rarely extended beyond the few blocks that a bicycle could take him. I played hooky that day; I had been sent to school as usual, met a friend on the way, and the two of us bought a pack of cigarettes—*Boules Américaines*—found an empty lot, and smoked. I had never been truant before; I had, needless to say, never smoked. I'd been a nice, obedient boy. But the things which sustained all that—those things had collapsed.

Perhaps it has always been that way; perhaps we know, and have always known, that stability and permanence are just literary or political fiction, that worlds are constantly coming to an end, and that men always wonder, as I did that morning, where they will be many years hence. But we have always assumed otherwise—always, that is, until modern war, revolution, and technology became not merely impositions on accepted patterns of life but the patterns themselves. On May 10, if I am correct, I became a member of a generation whose passion for loyalties was to be in constant tension with the world's inability to accept them. The things to which we attached ourselves had the fatal habit of crumbling under our clutches—families, nations, ideas, convictions, all had pitifully short lives which always left us looking for new homes and always willing, so far as strength and talent allowed, to forge new identities and seek new homes. The war itself was the greatest of our causes, not just for us who had escaped Hitler but for most Americans that I came to know during those years. None of us knew then that it was to be the last of the great causes and that the war itself represented not rectification and restoration but the beginning of an age which had to learn to take irony for granted. The great crusade turned into the Cold War and the threat of nuclear destruction—the permanence, that is, of change and annihilation. The assassinations of John Kennedy and Robert Kennedy and Martin Luther King, the failures of integration and the New Frontier, the war in Asia and its measured yet distinct steps of escalation—all these things came to be reminiscent of the morning of May 10. They were reminders of a past when I was not yet an American —not of other identities but of moments when identities and ideas were driven into exile. Each was a loud rap on the door, an awakening when bombs were falling and a world was coming to an end.

Becoming an American in New York was the second of many conversions. I had begun school in Luxembourg, had learned to speak its dialect, then converted to French in Brussels, then to English as spoken in Queens and Brooklyn. There were to be more conversions later, each of them cheerfully undertaken and, on the surface of things, successfully accomplished: the legacy of WASPiness of Amherst College in the early fifties, the drawl of west Texas, and then the growing suspicion that no voice, no style—no matter how great its attractions—was either central or safe from assault, and that none was fully capable of absorbing outsiders who had known or could be identified with other things. For the few minority-group students (as things were defined twenty years ago), the initiation offered by an Ivy League college meant sublimation or rejection of ethnic styles; it required one to abandon his blackness or his Jewishness and to become, as much as possible, a WASP.

A good deal has begun to change in the intervening years: minorities (and especially blacks) are developing new forms of ethnic consciousness and power, and the "mainstream" has become less substantial and less attractive—still powerful as an economic and political force, but lacking cultural initiative. To be a genuine American, in other words, involved, at best, choices between versions of Americanism, and the choices, depending on skin color and previous conditions of servitude, were often limited. It was probably true when I went to college, and it is certainly true now: after some experience at the center— after what used to be called Americanization—there are new flirtations with the periphery. The third generation (in state of mind, if not in order of birth) tries to establish its special place or find once more its forgotten ethnic roots. Despite the rhetoric of the melting pot, we are still a pluralistic nation, more pluralistic now, perhaps, than we were twenty years ago. To live or to grow up in America in 1970 is to search for a center which doesn't fully exist.

For almost half a century, at least since Ortega, we have

spoken with assurance and familiarity about mass culture without fully understanding what was meant. It is certainly true that traditions have been destroyed and rituals forgotten under the pressure of mass-media homogenization, bureaucracy, technology, and common public schools. And yet, if these things have tended to enervate the mainstream, as surely they have, and if they have tended to enforce compulsive consumerism and the anxieties of the good wife and mother, they have also created counter forces—new minorities, new voices, new cultures. Student revolt, black revolt, women's liberation, rock music, new dress and hair styles—none of these things is conceivable as it exists without some assistance from the media. The anger in Newark gives style and occasion to the anger in Detroit; black men may know that they are brothers, but television makes the anger visible and amplifies its expression. The media transmit the cataclysms that mark beginnings and ends, creating varieties of consciousness and style not only in space but in time—creating, in other words, successive states of mind as different as those of the varying cultures of isolated villages. There cannot be many sophisticated Americans who haven't felt at least once as I did on May 10, who have not had the sense that they are refugees of time and identity, if not of place.

To be a journalist is always to be an outsider, a man whose profession is distance. You are the perennial visitor, and after you've been at it for a while, you begin to carry the germs of Other Styles and Other Attitudes from place to place like a diseased sailor. Some town, some region, may still be home, but the tensions of estrangement die hard. And yet, I find it difficult to believe that this isn't more universally the American condition of the 1970's, not because Americans are always moving on—many, sometimes forgotten, do not—but because events and the forces

we have created, and which we honor, tend to displace
and destroy. *Things* move, even if we do not. The center
in which Americans always believed is beset by organizational and technological complexity; it becomes unmanageable, and we all become displaced persons, minorities
of outsiders whose alienation and anger vary only according to our willingness to resist the depersonalization that
technology imposes. One can retreat to a padded cell, or
to a suburb, or one can join the other refugees on their
various trips, or one can fight. We seek new homes, are
prepared to make new alliances, and enroll under new
banners: youth, drugs, civil rights, peace. For a moment
during the Cuban missile episode, and again in the days
after John F. Kennedy was killed, the national heartbeat
stopped, and we all sat at our television sets like Poles or
Belgians or Englishmen in their bomb shelters, wondering
what would be left when the raid was over, waiting for
the all-clear and the opportunity to resume life. And those
were not the first, nor were they to be the last moments
we would have to face it. A man who does it once learns
somehow that he will probably have to do it again. In
those moments we were all passionately together: our relations to each other didn't seem to change. And yet something else, something more subtle—a measure of confidence, an element of certainty—was lost. None of us felt
quite at home any more.

For people who chose this country as immigrants, dealing with the America of 1970 is simultaneously easier and
harder than for those whose ancestors arrived long ago.
To the extent that we were aware of what had been, we
were used to displacement, believing we were not inno-
cents of time or place or politics. But we had also made
a choice, even if that choice had often been forced upon
us by fascism or economic necessity: we embraced ideas,

traditions, loyalties which other Americans presumably took for granted. Now we discover—all of us—that here, too, there was fraud and self-deception, that Nuremberg may not have been justice but vengeance, and that the high ideals we wanted so much to profess existed alongside the most blatant racism and the most brutal kinds of human degradation. It was Americans who found the bones—and it will be to the nation's everlasting credit that they did—and it is Americans who are trying to rectify the injustices and compensate the victims. *We* discovered Mylai, and it was our kids who tried to stop the war, to fight discrimination and to battle the hunger and poverty of others. But the bones exist nonetheless, and the claims are still unpaid.

Again it feels like the tenth of May. We have had no end of speculation—analyses of the sixties, speculations about the seventies, the ritual of the decades—but in this case the accidents of the calendar seem to coincide with a more fundamental sense of change. The high hopes of the Kennedy and early Johnson years—the integrative, unifying possibilities of the New Frontier and Great Society, however illusory—have collapsed and are now disparaged by the very people who helped destroy them. We may never see such a time again. The danger now is that the center—what we used to call the mainstream and which Richard Nixon traduced into a "silent (read 'acquiescent') majority"—will be maintained artificially through intimidation and repression, through subtle coercion of the media and overt coercion by the police. If television can help unify isolated pockets of resistance, it can also divide and destroy, or simply neglect. The New Left's occasional rhetoric about fascism is inappropriate, at least for the moment, but the government-sanctioned attacks on dissent, on the young, on blacks, and on other minorities of assertion are real. One wonders whether the chill wind of a limited recession cannot be used by any cynical government as an instrument of political control—make jobs hard to get and institutional conformity is easier to enforce—and whether campaigns to improve the "environment," no matter how necessary and how nobly intended, will not be used like suburban zoning laws to protect the privileges and surroundings of those who have, against the demands and depredations of those who have not.

Somehow we are trying to restore the things we have lost through the semblance of action—to build, as it were, a center of plastic. We will invent or promote new problems to solve so that we can disregard old ones; we will try to divert people from the peace movement to pollution control and use the same tactics of engagement; we will speak about cleaning up streams so that we can forget the rats and crowding of the ghetto; we will launch noble campaigns against abstract enemies because the real enemies—the beneficiaries of exploitation, technology and war—are too powerful to offend. We will pretend that this is one nation managing its common problems when, in fact, it is a nation of strangely apprehensive people who are offered everything but a sense of continuity and a hopeful future.

The cultural energy of America has come, increasingly, from the periphery, from people who know they are outsiders, and who think of themselves as *others:* Jews, blacks, Catholics, kids, and all the rest. Perhaps it has always been that way, and yet there was, without doubt, a time when we believed that the future was with the nation, when we did not speak about "the silent majority" but rather about the common people, and when being outside was supposed to be a temporary condition, something that would be solved by mobility, opportunity, or integration. A generation ago America still seemed unique in this respect; we regarded our discontinuities as signs of progress: other things being equal, change was always for the better. This is what distinguished us not only from Europe but from most traditional societies where tomorrow was inevitably like today and where the shocks of time were generally catastrophic. Everywhere but here, history was the enemy of man. This is what made America simultaneously so attractive and so infuriating to those Europeans who understood the innocence in our idealism.

As a nation, we seemed to control our history and destiny, and it is this which we have lost. We have become a country of outsiders precisely because the world—at home and everywhere else—seems no longer manageable. This is why the anemic symbols of triumph are, at the same time, so overmanaged and so unsatisfactory, why the moon shot, for example, affects little except the television schedule, changes no lives, creates no hope, and produces no action. If there had ever been a center, a mainstream of ideas and action, it rested in the belief that things were manageable, and that all men and all things would participate. When that seems no longer possible, two things occur simultaneously: people drop out to do their own thing (or nothing) and those entrusted with management try to invent (or enforce) conditions and problems that make their stewardship appear successful. We do not end the war, but pretend that it no longer exists or that it has been forgotten; we do not eliminate poverty but disregard it; we do not risk hope that may remain unfulfilled, but take hope away.

If there is anything characteristic about the liberals of my generation it is that we have become trapped between our idealism about older institutions and ideas and our realization that something is desperately and perhaps even

fatally wrong. We see Spiro Agnew or Judge Julius Hoff-
man of Chicago as symbols of aberration, not as representatives of the system, but we are no longer sure. We
know that we have seen forms of repression far worse
than anything that exists in this country, but we can
easily imagine the events that might lead from here to
there. We now share with all conservatives a suspicion if
not of history then of the assumed beneficence of change.
At the same time, we cannot leave things alone, for if we
did we wouldn't be what we are, would be ideologically
unemployed. We are still, in other words, prepared to
join, to embrace, to support, and it is this, I think, that
distresses us most about those who, a few years ago, embarrassed us with their commitment, their willingness to
put their faith and bodies on the line, and who now seem
to have resigned so much.

But we also share something with all other Americans,
and that is our un-Americanism, which is to say our loss
of confidence. Americans, as I suggested earlier, have
always been, in some sense, out of place, living through
the tensions between regional and national citizenship,
between things accomplished and things undone, between
promises extended—equality, justice, opportunity—and
promises fulfilled. But through all this the belief in our
national citizenship—its ideals, its mythology, its expectations—remained vital and alive. We were in tension with
what we believed existed, not with what we suspected had
ceased to be.

There was, moreover, place itself. It was possible to leave
home, but it was not enforced. Even if *things* changed,
landmarks were supposed to remain as reminders of another time, as symbols of permanence and tradition. Now
the bulldozers of modernization invade the neighborhood
like tanks, the high-rise replaces the brownstone, the

supermarket drives out the corner store, the cotton picker and the automatic machine uproot, divide, and transform. Men are driven from their places; we have evicted ourselves.

Perhaps it can all be restored, perhaps there will be new crusades which can enlist volunteers of high ideals, perhaps even "the environment" will be more than an artificial campaign to make things look good, to deodorize the john and purify the water. For the moment it looks desperately doubtful. The ravages in Vietnam suggest that our passion for the air and the earth may be more proprietary than humane, and our tolerance of poverty and hunger, foreign and domestic, is hardly a sign of hope. We have all had our tenth of May, but for Americans the effect has been, perhaps, more shattering than for all others. We had all been believers, believers in ourselves and hence in the future. But events have driven a barrier between the past and the present, and we are now all refugees in our own country.

THE FORGOTTEN AMERICAN

*"You better pay attention to the
son of a bitch before he burns
the country down."*

There is hardly a language
to describe him, or even a set of social statistics.
Just names: racist-bigot-redneck-ethnic-Irish-Italian-Pole-
Hunkie-Yahoo. The lower middle class. A blank. The man
under whose hat lies the great American desert. Who
watches the tube, plays the horses, and keeps the niggers
out of his union and his neighborhood. Who might vote
for Wallace (but didn't). Who cheers when the cops beat
up on demonstrators. Who is free, white, and twenty-one,
has a job, a home, a family, and is up to his eyeballs in
credit. In the guise of the working class—or the American

yeoman or John Smith—he was once the hero of the civics book, the man that Andrew Jackson called "the bone and sinew of the country." Now he is "the forgotten man," perhaps the most alienated person in America.

Nothing quite fits, except perhaps omission and semi-invisibility. America is supposed to be divided between affluence and poverty, between slums and suburbs. John Kenneth Galbraith begins the foreword to *The Affluent Society* with the phrase, "Since I sailed for Switzerland in the early summer of 1955 to begin work on this book . . ." But *between* slums and suburbs, between Scarsdale and Harlem, between Wellesley and Roxbury, between Shaker Heights and Hough, there are some eighty million people (depending on how you count them) who didn't sail for Switzerland in the summer of 1955, or at any other time, and who never expect to. Between slums and suburbs: South Boston and South San Francisco, Bell and Parma, Astoria and Bay Ridge, Newark, Cicero, Downey, Daly City, Charlestown, Flatbush. Union halls, American Legion posts, neighborhood bars and bowling leagues, the Ukrainian Club and the Holy Name. Main Street. To try to describe all this is like trying to describe America itself. If you look for it, you find it everywhere: the rows of frame houses overlooking the belching steel mills in Bethlehem, Pennsylvania, two-family brick houses in Canarsie (where the most common slogan, even in the middle of a political campaign is "Curb your dog"); the Fords and Chevies with a decal American flag on the rear window (usually a cut-out from the *Reader's Digest*, and displayed in counter-protest against peaceniks and "those bastards who carry Vietcong flags in demonstrations"); the bunting on the porch rail with the inscription, "Welcome Home, Pete." The gold star in the window.

When he was Under Secretary of Housing and Urban

Development, Robert C. Wood tried a definition. It is not good, but it's the best we have:

> He is a white employed male . . . earning between $5,000 and $10,000. He works regularly, steadily, dependably, wearing a blue collar or white collar. Yet the frontiers of his career expectations have been fixed since he reached the age of thirty-five, when he found that he had too many obligations, too much family, and too few skills to match opportunities with aspirations.
>
> This definition of the "working American" involves almost 23-million American families.
>
> The working American lives in the gray area fringes of a central city or in a close-in or very far-out cheaper suburban subdivision of a large metropolitan area. He is likely to own a home and a car, especially as his income begins to rise. Of those earning between $6,000 and $7,500, 70 percent own their own homes and 94 percent drive their own cars.
>
> 94 percent have no education beyond high school and 43 percent have only completed the eighth grade.

He does all the right things, obeys the law, goes to church and insists—usually—that his kids get a better education than he had. But the right things don't seem to be paying off. While he is making more than he ever made—perhaps more than he'd ever dreamed—he's still struggling while a lot of others—"them" (on welfare, in demonstrations, in the ghettos)—are getting most of the attention. "I'm working my ass off," a guy tells you on a stoop in South Boston. "My kids don't have a place to swim, my parks are full of glass, and I'm supposed to bleed for a bunch of people on relief." In New York a man who drives a Post Office trailer truck at night (4:00 P.M to midnight) and a cab during the day (7:00 A.M to 2:00 P.M.), and who hustles radios for his Post Office buddies on the side, is ready, as he says, to "knock somebody's ass." "The colored guys work when they feel like it. Sometimes they show up and sometimes they don't. One guy tore up all the time cards. I'd like to see a white guy do that and get away with it."

Nobody knows how many people in America moonlight (half of the eighteen million families in the $5,000 to $10,000 bracket have two or more wage earners) or how many have to hustle on the side. "I don't think anybody has a single job any more," said Nicholas Kisburg, the research director for a Teamsters Union Council in New York. "All the cops are moonlighting, and the teachers; and there's a million guys who are hustling, guys with phony social security numbers who are hiding part of what they make so they don't get kicked out of a housing project, or guys who work as guards at sports events and get free meals that they don't want to pay taxes on. Every one of them is cheating. They are underground people— *Untermenschen*. . . . We really have no systematic data on any of this. We have no ideas of the attitudes of the white worker. (We've been too busy studying the black worker.) And yet he's the source of most of the reaction in this country."

The reaction is directed at almost every visible target: at integration and welfare, taxes and sex education, at the rich and the poor, the foundations and students, at the "smart people in the suburbs." In New York State the legislature cuts the welfare budget; in Los Angeles, the voters reelect Yorty after a whispered racial campaign against the Negro favorite. In Minneapolis a police detective named Charles Stenvig, promising "to take the handcuffs off the police," is elected mayor by a margin stunning even to his supporters: in Massachusetts the voters mail tea bags to their representatives in protest against new taxes, and in state after state legislatures are passing bills to punish student demonstrators. ("We keep talking about permissiveness in training kids," said a Los Angeles labor official, "but we forget that these are our kids.")

And yet all these things are side manifestations of a malaise that lacks a language. Whatever law and order means, for example, to a man who feels his wife is unsafe on the street after dark or in the park at any time, or whose kids get shaken down in the school yard, it also means something like normality—the demand that everybody play it by the book, that cultural and social standards be somehow restored to their civics-book simplicity, that things shouldn't be as they are but as they were supposed to be. If there is a revolution in this country—a revolt in manners, standards of dress and obscenity, and, more important, in our official sense of what America is—there is also a counter-revolt. Sometimes it is inarticulate, and sometimes (perhaps most of the time) people are either too confused or apathetic—or simply too polite and too decent—to declare themselves. In Astoria, Queens, a white working-class district of New York, people who make $7,000 or $8,000 a year (sometimes in two jobs) call themselves affluent, even though the Bureau of Labor Statistics regards an income of less than $9,500 in New York inadequate to a moderate standard of living. And in a similar neighborhood in Brooklyn a truck driver who earns $151 a week tells you he's doing well, living in a two-story frame house separated by a narrow driveway from similar houses, thousands of them in block after block. This year, for the first time, he will go on a cruise—he and his wife and two other couples—two weeks in the Caribbean. He

went to work after World War II ($57 a week) and he has
lived in the same house for twenty years, accumulating
two television sets, wall-to-wall carpeting in a small living
room, and a basement that he recently remodeled into a
recreation room with the help of two moonlighting firemen. "We get fairly good salaries, and this is a good
neighborhood, one of the few good ones left. We have no
smoked Irishmen around."

Stability is what counts, stability in job and home and
neighborhood, stability in the church and in friends. At
night you watch television and sometimes on a weekend
you go to a nice place—maybe a downtown hotel—for dinner with another couple. (Or maybe your sister, or maybe
bowling, or maybe, if you're defeated, a night at the track.)
The wife has the necessary appliances, often still being
paid off, and the money you save goes for your daughter's
orthodontist, and later for her wedding. The smoked
Irishmen—the colored (no one says black; few even say
Negro)—represent change and instability, kids who cause
trouble in school, who get treatment that your kids never
got, that you never got. ("Those fucking kids," they tell
you in South Boston, "raising hell, and not one of 'em
paying his own way. Their fucking mothers are all on welfare.") The black kids mean a change in the rules, a
double standard in grades and discipline, and—vaguely—a
challenge to all you believed right. Law and order is the
stability and predictability of established ways. Law and
order is equal treatment—in school, in jobs, in the courts—
even if you're cheating a little yourself. The Forgotten
Man is Jackson's man. He is the vestigial American democrat of 1840: "They all know that their success depends
upon their own industry and economy and that they must
not expect to become suddenly rich by the fruits of

their toil." He is also Franklin Roosevelt's man—the man
whose vote (or whose father's vote) sustained the New
Deal.

There are other considerations, other styles, other problems. A postman in a Charlestown (Boston) housing project: eight children and a ninth on the way. Last year, by
working overtime, his income went over $7,000. This year,
because he reported it, the Housing Authority is raising
his rent from $78 to $106 a month, a catastrophe for a
family that pays $2.20 a day for milk, has never had a
vacation, and for which an excursion is "going out for ice
cream." "You try and save for something better; we hope
to get out of here to someplace where the kids can play,
where there's no broken glass, and then something always
comes along that knocks you right back. It's like being at
the bottom of the well waiting for a guy to throw you a
rope." The description becomes almost Chaplinesque. Life
is humble but not simple; the terrors of insolent bureaucracies and contemptuous officials produce a demonology
that loses little of its horror for being partly misunderstood. You want to get a sink fixed but don't want to
offend the manager; want to get an eye operation that
may (or may not) have been necessitated by a military
injury five years earlier, "but the Veterans Administration
says I signed away my benefits"; want to complain to
someone about the teen-agers who run around breaking
windows and harassing women but get no response either
from the management or the police. "You're afraid to
complain because if they don't get you during the day
they'll get you at night." Automobiles, windows, children,
all become hostages to the vague terrors of everyday life;
everything is vulnerable. Liabilities that began long ago
cannot possibly be liquidated: "I never learned anything
in that school except how to fight. I got tired of being

caned by the teachers so at sixteen I quit and joined the
Marines. I still don't know anything."

American culture? Wealth is visible, and so, now, is
poverty. Both have become intimidating clichés. But the
rest? A vast, complex, and disregarded world that was
once—in belief, and in fact—the American middle: Grey-
hound and Trailways bus terminals in little cities at midnight, each of them with its neon lights and its cardboard
hamburgers; acres of tar-paper beach bungalows in places
like Revere and Rockaway; the hair curlers in the supermarket on Saturday, and the little girls in the communion
dresses the next morning; pinball machines and the *Daily
News*, the *Reader's Digest* and Ed Sullivan; houses with
tiny front lawns (or even large ones) adorned with statues
of the Virgin or of Sambo welcomin' de folks home; Clint
Eastwood or Julie Andrews at the Palace; the trotting
tracks and the dog tracks—Aurora Downs, Connaught
Park, Roosevelt, Yonkers, Rockingham, and forty others—
where gray men come not for sport and beauty, but to
read numbers, to study and dope. (If you win you have
figured something, have in a small way controlled your
world, have surmounted your impotence. If you lose, bad
luck, shit. "I'll break his goddamned head.") Baseball is
not the national pastime; racing is. For every man who
goes to a major-league baseball game there are four who
go to the track and probably four more who go to the
candy store or the barbershop to make their bets. (Total
track attendance in 1965: 62 million plus another 10 million who went to the dogs.)

There are places, and styles, and attitudes. If there are
neighborhoods of aspiration, suburban enclaves for the
mobile young executive and the aspiring worker, there are
also places of limited expectation and dead-end districts

where mobility is finished. But even there you can often find, however vestigial, a sense of place, the roots of old ethnic loyalties, and a passionate, if often futile, battle against intrusion and change. "Everybody around here," you are told, "pays his own way." In this world the problems are not the ABM or air pollution (have they heard of Biafra?) or the international population crisis; the problem is to get your street cleaned, your garbage collected, to get your husband home from Vietnam alive; to negotiate installment payments and to keep the schools orderly. Ask anyone in Scarsdale or Winnetka about the schools and they'll tell you about new programs, or about how many are getting into Harvard, or about the teachers. Ask in Oakland or the North Side of Chicago, and they'll tell you that they have (or haven't) had trouble; somewhere in his gut the man in those communities knows that mobility and choice in this society are limited. He cannot imagine any major change for the better; but he can imagine change for the worse. And yet for a decade he is the one who has been asked to carry the burden of social reform, to integrate his schools and his neighborhood, has been asked by comfortable people to pay the social debts due to the poor and the black. In Boston, in San Francisco, in Chicago (not to mention Newark or Oakland) he has been telling the reformers to go to hell. The Jewish schoolteachers of New York and the Irish parents of Dorchester have asked the same question: "What the hell did Lindsay (or the Beacon Hill Establishment) ever do for us?"

The ambiguities and changes in American life that occupy discussions in university seminars and policy debates in Washington, and that form the backbone of contemporary popular sociology, become increasingly the conditions of trauma and frustration in the middle. Although the New Frontier and Great Society contained some programs for those not already on the rolls of social pathology—federal aid for higher education, for example— the public priorities and the rhetoric contained little. The emphasis, properly, was on the poor, on the inner cities (*e.g.*, Negroes) and the unemployed. But in Chicago a widow with three children who earns $7,000 a year can't get them college loans because she makes too much; the money is reserved for people on relief. New schools are built in the ghetto but not in the white working-class neighborhoods where they are just as dilapidated. In Newark the head of a white vigilante group (now a city councilman) runs, among other things, on a platform opposing pro-Negro discrimination. "When pools are being built in the Central Ward—don't they think white kids have got frustration? The white can't get a job; we have to hire Negroes first." The middle class, said Congressman Roman Pucinski of Illinois, who represents a lot of it, "is in revolt. Everyone has been generous in supporting anti-poverty. Now the middle-class American is disqualified from most of the programs."

The frustrated middle. The liberal wisdom about welfare, ghettos, student revolt, and Vietnam has only a marginal place, if any, for the values and life of the working man. It flies in the face of most of what he was taught to cherish and respect: hard work, order, authority, self-reliance. He fought, either alone or through labor organizations, to establish the precincts he now considers his own. Union seniority, the civil service bureaucracy, and the petty professionalism established by the merit system in the public schools become sinecures of particular ethnic groups or of those who have learned to negotiate and master the system. A man who worked all his life to accumulate the points and grades and paraphernalia to

become an assistant school principal (no matter how silly
the requirements) is not likely to relinquish his position
with equanimity. Nor is a dock worker whose only estate
is his longshoreman's card. The job, the points, the credits
become property:

> Some men leave their sons money [wrote a union mem-
> ber to the *New York Times*], some large investments,
> some business connections, and some a profession. I have
> only one worthwhile thing to give: my trade. I hope to
> follow a centuries-old tradition and sponsor my sons for an
> apprenticeship. For this simple father's wish it is said that
> I discriminate against Negroes. Don't all of us discrim-
> inate? Which of us . . . will not choose a son over all
> others?

Suddenly the rules are changing—all the rules. If you
protect your job for your own you may be called a bigot.
At the same time it's perfectly acceptable to shout black
power and to endorse it. What does it take to be a good
American? *Give the black man a position because he is
black, not because he necessarily works harder or does
the job better.* What does it take to be a good American?
Dress nicely, hold a job, be clean-cut, don't judge a man
by the color of his skin or the country of his origin. What
about the demands of Negroes, the long hair of the students, the dirty movies, the people who burn draft cards
and American flags? Do you have to go out in the street
with picket signs, do you have to burn the place down to
get what you want? What does it take to be a good
American? *This is a sick society, a racist society, we are
fighting an immoral war.* ("I'm against the Vietnam war,
too," says the truck driver in Brooklyn. "I see a good kid
come home with half an arm and a leg in a brace up to
here, and what's it all for? I was glad to see *my kid* flunk

the Army physical. Still, somebody has to say no to these demonstrators and enforce the law.") What does it take to be a good American?

The conditions of trauma and frustration in the middle. What does it take to be a good American? Suddenly there are demands for Italian power and Polish power and Ukrainian power. In Cleveland the Poles demand a seat on the school board, and get it, and in Pittsburgh John Pankuch, the seventy-three-year-old president of the National Slovak Society demands "action, plenty of it to make up for lost time." Black power is supposed to be nothing but emulation of the ways in which other ethnic groups made it. But have they made it? In Reardon's Bar on East 8th Street in South Boston where the workmen come for their fish-chowder lunch and for their rye and ginger, they still identify themselves as Galway men and Kilkenny men; at the newsstand in Astoria you can buy *Il Progresso, El Tiempo,* the *Staats-Zeitung,* the *Irish World,* plus papers in Greek, Hungarian, and Polish. At the parish of Our Lady of Mount Carmel the priests hear confession in English, Italian, and Spanish and, nearby, the biggest attraction is not the stickball game, but the *bocce* court. Some of the poorest people in America are white, native, and have lived all of their lives in the same place as their fathers and grandfathers. The problems that were presumably solved in some distant past, in that prehistoric era before the textbooks were written—problems of assimilation, of upward mobility—now turn out to be very much unsolved. The melting pot and all: millions made it, millions moved to the affluent suburbs; several million—no one knows how many—did not. The median income in Irish South Boston is $5,100 a year but the community-action workers have a hard time convincing the local citizens that any white man who is not stupid or irresponsible can be poor. Pride still keeps them from applying for income supplements or Medicaid, but it does not keep them from resenting those who do. In Pittsburgh, where the members of Polish-American organizations earn an estimated $5,000 to $6,000 (and some fall below the poverty line), the Poverty Programs are nonetheless directed primarily to Negroes, and almost everywhere the thing called urban backlash associates itself in some fashion with ethnic groups whose members have themselves only a precarious hold on the security of affluence. Almost everywhere in the old cities, tribal neighborhoods and their styles are under assault by masscult. The Italian grocery gives way to the supermarket, the ma-and-pa store and the walk-up are attacked by urban renewal. And almost everywhere, that assault tends to depersonalize and to alienate. It has always been this way, but with time the brave new world that replaces old patterns becomes increasingly bureaucratized, distant, and hard to control.

Yet beyond the problems of ethnic identity, beyond the problems of Poles and Irishmen left behind, there are others more pervasive and more dangerous. For every Greek or Hungarian there are a dozen American-Americans who are past ethnic consciousness and who are as alienated, as confused, and as angry as the rest. The obvious manifestations are the same everywhere—race, taxes, welfare, students—but the threat seems invariably more cultural and psychological than economic or social. What upset the police at the Chicago convention most was not so much the politics of the demonstrators as their manners and their hair. (The barbershops in their neighborhoods don't advertise Beatle Cuts but the Flat Top and the Chicago Box.) The affront comes from middle-class people—and their children—who had been cast in the role of social exemplars (and from those cast as unfortunates worthy of public charity) who offend all the things on which working class identity is built: "hippies [said a San Francisco longshoreman] who fart around the streets and don't work"; welfare recipients who strike and march for better treatment; "all those [said a California labor official] who challenge the precepts that these people live on." If ethnic groups are beginning to organize to get theirs, so are others: police and firemen ("The cop is the new nigger"); schoolteachers; lower-middle-class housewives fighting sex education and bussing; small property owners who have no ethnic communion but a passionate interest in lower taxes, more policemen, and stiffer penalties for criminals. In San Francisco the Teamsters, who had never been known for such interests before, recently demonstrated in support of the police and law enforcement and, on another occasion, joined a group called Mothers Support Neighborhood Schools at a school-board meeting to oppose—with their presence and later, apparently, with their fists—a proposal to integrate the schools through bussing. ("These people," someone said at the meeting, "do not look like mothers.")

Which is not to say that all is frustration and anger, that anybody is ready "to burn the country down." They are not even ready to elect standard-model demagogues. "A lot of labor people who thought of voting for Wallace were ashamed of themselves when they realized what they were about to do," said Morris Iushewitz, an officer of New York's Central Labor Council. Because of a massive last-minute union campaign, and perhaps for other reasons, the blue-collar vote for Wallace fell far below the figures predicted by the early polls last fall. Any number of people, moreover, who are not doing well by any set of official statistics, who are earning well below the national mean ($8,000 a year), or who hold two jobs to stay above it, think of themselves as affluent, and often use that word. It is almost as if not to be affluent is to be un-American. People who can't use the word tend to be angry; people who come too close to those who can't become frightened. The definition of affluence is generally pinned to what comes in, not to the quality of life as it's lived. The $8,000 son of a man who never earned more than $4,500 may, for that reason alone, believe that he's "doing all right." If life is not all right, if he can't get his curbs fixed, or his streets patrolled, if the highways are crowded and the beaches polluted, if the schools are ineffectual, he is still able to call himself affluent, feels, perhaps, a social compulsion to do so. His anger, if he is angry, is not that of the wage earner resenting management—and certainly not that of the socialist ideologue asking for redistribution of wealth—but that of the consumer, the taxpayer, and the family man. (Inflation and taxes are wiping out most of the wage gains made in labor contracts signed during the past three years.) Thus he will vote for a Louise Day Hicks in Boston who promises to hold the color line in the schools or for a Charles Stenvig calling for law enforcement in Minneapolis but reject a George Wallace who seems to threaten his pocketbook. The danger is that he will identify with the politics of the Birchers and other middle-class reactionaries (who often pretend to speak for him) even though his income and style of life are far removed from theirs: that taxes, for example, will be identified with welfare rather than war, and that he will blame his limited means on the small slice of the poor rather than the fat slice of the rich.

If you sit and talk to people like Marjorie Lemlow, who heads Mothers Support Neighborhood Schools in San Francisco, or Joe Owens, a house painter who is president of a community-action organization in Boston, you quickly discover that the roots of reaction and the roots of reform are often identical, and that the response to particular situations is more often contingent on the programs of the politicians and leaders who appear to care than on the conditions of life or the ideology of the victims. Mrs. Lemlow wants to return the schools to some virtuous past; she worries about disintegration of the family and she speaks vaguely about something that she can't bring herself to call a conspiracy against Americanism. She has been accused of leading a bunch of Birchers, and she sometimes talks Birch language. But whatever the form, her sense of things comes from a small-town vision of national virtues and her unhappiness from the assaults of urban sophistication. It just so happens that a lot of reactionaries now sing that tune, and that the liberals are indifferent.

Joe Owens—probably because of his experience as a Head Start parent, and because of his association with an effective community-action program—talks a different language. He knows, somehow, that no simple past can be restored. In his world the villains are not conspirators but bureaucrats and politicians, and he is beginning to discover that in a struggle with officials the black man in the ghetto and the working man (black or white) have the same problems. "Every time you ask for something from the politicians they treat you like a beggar, like you ought to be grateful for what you have. They try to make you feel ashamed."

The imponderables are youth and tradition and change. The civics book and the institution it celebrates—however passé—still hold the world together. The revolt is in their name, not against them. And there is simple decency, the language and practice of the folksy cliché, the small town,

the Boy Scout virtues, the neighborhood charity, the ob-
ligation to support the church, the rhetoric of open opportunity: "They can keep Wallace and they can keep
Alabama. We didn't fight a dictator for four years so we
could elect one over here." What happens when all that
becomes Mickey Mouse? Is there an urban ethic to replace the values of the small town? Is there a coherent
public philosophy, a consistent set of beliefs to replace
family, home, and hard work? What happens when the
hang-ups of upper-middle-class kids are in fashion and
those of blue-collar kids are not? What happens when
"do your own thing" becomes not the slogan of the soli-
tary deviant but the norm? Is it possible that as the institutions and beliefs of tradition are fashionably denigrated
a blue-collar generation gap will open to the Right as well
as to the Left? (There is statistical evidence, for example,
that Wallace's greatest support within the unions came
from people who are between twenty-one and twenty-
nine, those, that is, who have the most tenuous association with the liberalism of labor.) Most are politically
silent; although SDS has been trying to organize blue-
collar high school students, there are no Mario Savios or
Mark Rudds—either of the Right or the Left—among them.
At the same time the union leaders, some of them old
hands from the Thirties, aren't sure that the kids are following them either. Who speaks for the son of the longshoreman or the Detroit auto worker? What happens if
he doesn't get to college? What, indeed, happens when he
does?

Vaguely but unmistakably the hopes that a youth-
worshiping nation historically invested in its young are
becoming threats. We have never been unequivocal about
the symbolic patricide of Americanization and upward
mobility, but if at one time mobility meant rejection of

older (or European) styles it was, at least, done in the name of America. Now the labels are blurred and the objectives indistinct. Just at the moment when a tradition-bound Italian father is persuaded that he should send his sons to college—that education is the only future—the college blows up. At the moment when a parsimonious taxpayer begins to shell out for what he considers an extravagant state university system the students go on strike. Marijuana, sexual liberation, dress style, draft resistance, even the rhetoric of change become monsters and demons in a world that appears to turn old virtues upside down. The paranoia that fastened on Communism twenty years ago (and sometimes still does) is increasingly directed to vague conspiracies undermining the schools, the family, order, and discipline. "They're feeding the kids this generation-gap business," says a Chicago housewife who grinds out a campaign against sex education on a duplicating machine in her living room. "The kids are told to make their own decisions. They're all mixed up by situation ethics and open-ended questions. They're alienating children from their own parents." They? The churches, the schools, even the YMCA and the Girl Scouts, are implicated. But a major share of the villainy is now also attributed to "the social science centers," to the apostles of sensitivity training, and to what one California lady, with some embarrassment, called "nude therapy." "People with sane minds are being altered by psychological methods." The current major campaign of the John Birch Society is not directed against Communists in government or the Supreme Court, but against sex education.

(There is, of course, also sympathy with the young, especially in poorer areas where kids have no place to play. "Everybody's got to have a hobby," a South Boston adolescent told a youth worker. "Ours is throwing rocks."

If people will join reactionary organizations to protect their children, they will also support others: community-action agencies which help kids get jobs, Head Start parent groups, Boys Clubs. "Getting this place cleaned up" sometimes refers to a fear of young hoods; sometimes it points to the day when there is a park or a playground or when the existing park can be used. "I want to see them grow up to have a little fun.")

Beneath it all there is a more fundamental ambivalence, not only about the young, but about institutions—the schools, the churches, the Establishment—and about the future itself. In the major cities of the East (though perhaps not in the West) there is a sense that time is against you, that one is living "in one of the few decent neighborhoods left," that "if I can get $125 a week upstate (or downstate) I'll move." The institutions that were supposed to mediate social change and which, more than ever, are becoming priesthoods of information and conglomerates of social engineers, are increasingly suspect. To attack the Ford Foundation (as Wright Patman has done) is not only to fan the embers of historic populism against concentrations of wealth and power, but also to arouse those who feel that they are trapped by an alliance of upper-class WASPs and lower-class Negroes. If the foundations have done anything for the blue-collar worker he doesn't seem to be aware of it. At the same time the distrust of professional educators that characterizes the black militants is becoming increasingly prevalent among a minority of lower-middle-class whites who are beginning to discover that the schools aren't working for them either. ("Are all those new programs just a cover-up for failure?") And if the Catholic Church is under attack from its liberal members (on birth control, for example) it is also alienating the traditionalists who liked their minor saints (even if they didn't actually exist) and were perfectly content with the Latin Mass. For the alienated Catholic liberal there are other places to go; for the lower-middle-class parishioner in Chicago or Boston there are none.

Perhaps, in some measure, it has always been this way. Perhaps none of this is new. And perhaps it is also true that the American lower middle has never had it so good. And yet surely there is a difference, and that is that the common man has lost his visibility and, somehow, his claim on public attention. There are old liberals and so-cialists—men like Michael Harrington—who believe that a new alliance can be forged for progressive social action:

> From Marx to Mills, the Left has regarded the middle class as a stratum of hypocritical, vacillating rear-guarders. There was often sound reason for this contempt. But is it not possible that a new class is coming into being? It is not the old middle class of small property owners and entrepreneurs, nor the new middle class of managers. It is composed of scientists, technicians, teachers, and pro-fessionals in the public sector of the society. By education and work experience it is predisposed toward planning. It could be an ally of the poor and the organized workers— or their sophisticated enemy. In other words, an unprec-edented social and political variable seems to be taking shape in America.
>
> The American worker, even when he waits on a table or holds open a door, is not servile; he does not carry him-self like an inferior. The openness, frankness, and demo-cratic manner which Tocqueville described in the last century persists to this very day. They have been a source of rudeness, contemptuous ignorance, violence—and of a creative self-confidence among great masses of people. It was in this latter spirit that the CIO was organized and the black freedom movement marched.

There are recent indications that the white lower-middle class is coming back on the roster of public priorities. Pucinski tells you that liberals in Congress are privately discussing the pressure from the middle class. There are proposals now to increase personal income-tax exemptions from $600 to $1000 (or $1,200) for each dependent, to protect all Americans with a national insurance system covering catastrophic medical expenses, and to put a floor under all incomes. Yet these things by themselves are insufficient. Nothing is sufficient without a national sense of restoration. What Pucinski means by the middle class has, in some measure, always been represented. A physician earning $75,000 a year is also a working man but he is hardly a victim of the welfare system. Nor, by and large, are the stockholders of the Standard Oil Company or U.S. Steel. The fact that American ideals have often been corrupted in the cause of self-aggrandizement does not make them any less important for the cause of social reform and justice. "As a movement with the conviction that there is more for people than greed and fear," Harrington said, "the Left must . . . also speak in the name of the historic idealism of the United States."

The issue, finally, is not *the program* but the vision, the angle of view. A huge constituency may be coming up for grabs, and there is considerable evidence that its political mobility is more sensitive than anyone can imagine, that all the sociological determinants are not as significant as the simple facts of concern and leadership. When Robert Kennedy was killed last year, thousands of working-class people who had expected to vote for him—if not hundreds of thousands—shifted their loyalties to Wallace. A man who can change from a progressive democrat into a bigot overnight deserves attention.

[1969]

GROWING UP ON MECHANIC STREET

It is impossible to think of those adolescents without a strange mixture of affection, apprehension and fear. To imagine them at all it becomes necessary to shoulder aside the black/white clichés of youth talk—about middle-class revolt and ghetto rebellion —and to perceive a grayer reality. I am not writing here of affluent suburbs or what others have called blacktown, but about the children of those whom Americans once celebrated as workingmen. (Again sociology fails us; there are no definitions or statistics. If there were, the matter would be better understood.)

They exist everywhere, but convention has almost wiped them from sight. They are not supposed to be there, are perhaps not really supposed to believe even in their own existence. Thus they function not for themselves but to define and affirm the position of others: those who are very poor or those who are affluent, those who go to college. In visiting the schools they attend, one must constantly define them not by what they are, but by what they are not, and sometimes, in talking to teachers and administrators, one begins to doubt whether they exist at all.

Phrases like "the forgotten man" and "the silent majority" are too political to use as normative descriptions, but there is no doubt that there are forgotten kids who are indeed genuine victims: children of factory workers and truck drivers, of shop foremen and salesclerks, kids who live in row houses above steel mills and in tacky developments at the edge of town, children who will not go to college, who will not become affluent, who will not march the streets, who will do no more, nor less, than relive the lives of their parents.

We have all seen them: the kids on the corner with their duck-tail haircuts; the canvas-bag-toting types, lonely and lost, lining up at the induction centers; kids in knocked-down cars which seem to have no springs in back —whose wedding announcements appear daily in the newspapers of small towns (Mr. Jones works for the New York Central Railroad—no particular job worth mentioning—Miss Smith is a senior at Washington High), and whose deaths are recorded in the weekly reports from Saigon—name, rank, hometown. On the south side of Bethlehem, Pennsylvania, just above the mills, there is an alley called Mechanic Street; once, it was the heart of the old immigrant district, the first residence of thousands of Hungarians, Russians, Poles, Mexicans, Germans, Czechs and Croats. Most of them have now moved on to materially better things, but they regard this as their ancestral home. Think of the children of Mechanic Street; think of places called Liberty High and South Boston High, of Central High and Charlestown High, and of hundreds of others where defeat does not enjoy the ironic distinction or the acknowledged injustice of racial oppression.

The fact that defeat is not universal makes the matter all the more ugly. The record of college placement and vocational success which schools so love to celebrate, and the occasional moments of triumphant self-realization which they do not, obscure—seem, in fact, to legitimize— the unexpressed vacancy, the accepted defeat, and the unspoken frustration around and beyond the fringe. We have a pernicious habit of confusing the beginning of a trend with its ultimate accomplishment: when we see a growing number of students from blue-collar families going to college we begin to assume that they will all be happy and successful when they get there. Yet it is still a fact, as it always was, that the lower ranks of the economic order have the smallest chance of sending their children on, and that those who fall below the academic middle in high school tend to represent a disproportionate percentage of poor and working-class families. It seems somehow redundant and unnecessary to say all this again; but if it isn't said, there will be no stopping the stories of blissful academic success.

The social order of most white high schools—the attitudes that teachers and students have about other students —is based (in proper democratic fashion) on what people do in school, on their interests, their clubs, their personalities, their accomplishments. (Students from blue-collar

families with serious college ambitions associate with the
children of white-collar professionals, and share their attitudes, styles, and beliefs, which tend to be more liberal
—politically and personally—than those of their parents. A
few participated in the Vietnam moratorium last fall, and
a handful, unknown to their fathers, have gone to the
local draft counselors if any were available. But they represent a minority.) It is possible to leave Mechanic Street
through school achievement—to community and state colleges, to technical schools, to better jobs—yet it is unlikely.
Fewer than half actually go. What kids do in school tends,
as always, to be predetermined. The honors class is filled
with the children of professionals, kids whose parents
have gone to college. The general course (meaning the
dead end) and the vocational track are composed of the
sons and daughters of blue-collar workers. The more "opportunity," the more justified the destiny of those who
are tagged for failure. The world accepts the legitimacy
of their position. And so do they. Their tragedy and the
accompanying threat lie precisely in their acceptance of
the low esteem in which school, society, and often their
parents regard them and their inability to learn a language to express what they feel but dare not trust.

*Imagine, says a school counselor, that you could become
an animal, any animal. What species would you choose?
The secret heart would choose freedom: eagles soaring
over mountains, mustangs running across the plain, grey-
hounds loping through fields. Freedom.*

Dreams are to be denied. The imagined future is like
the present without parents. Jobs, domesticity, children—
with little joy—seen in shades of gray. Coming out of
school in the afternoon the boys already resemble their
fathers when the shifts change—rows of dark, tufted mail-
order-house jackets, rows of winter hats with the earflaps

laced above the head, crossing the road from the plant to the parking lot, from the high school to the waiting buses and the bare-wheeled Chevvies. The girls, not yet stretched by pregnancy, often trim in short skirts and bright sweaters, will catch up with their mothers, will be married at eighteen or twenty, will often be engaged before the tedium of school is at an end. "Unwanted kids," says a school administrator, "kids of guys who got girls in trouble, kids of Korean War veterans and veterans of World War II, who didn't want the first child, and before they knew it they had two or three. All their lives their kids have been told to get out of the way, to go watch television. They don't have anybody to talk to. There was a recent survey that indicated that seventy-two percent of the first children of this generation were unwanted. These are the kids."

They sit in rows of five, five by five, in the classroom, existing from bell to bell, regurgitating answers, waiting for the next relief. The mindless lessons, the memory and boredom, and the stultifying order of cafeterias and study halls—no talking, sit straight, get a pass—these things need not be described again. From bell to bell: English, mathematics, history, science, and, for some, release to the more purposeful and engaging activities of the shop: auto mechanics, data processing, welding, wiring, carpentry and all the rest—some relevant, some obsolete, but all direct. There is an integrity, even joy, in material results— a sharp tool, an engine repaired, a solid joint—that the artificial world of the conventional academic course rarely allows. Material things respond, theory is applicable and comprehensible—either this thing works or it doesn't; it never prevaricates or qualifies, while words and social behavior, metaphors and politics, remain cloudy, elusive, and distant. You see them wiring an electric motor, or turning a machine part, a lathe, or fixing a car: pleasure, engagement or, better, a moment of truth. The Big Lie, if there is one, will be revealed later. ("No," says the director of a vocational school in an industrial city, "We don't tell the students that the construction unions are hard to join; it would discourage them in their work. They'll find out soon enough that it helps to know someone, to have a father or an uncle in the union . . . But after a kid manages to break in, he's proud of what he learned in the school of hard knocks, and he'll do the same thing to the new guys.")

From class to class, from school to home and back, there is a sort of passing-through. What is learned is to defer—to time, to authority, to events. One keeps asking, "What do they want, what do they do, what do they dream about?" and the answer is almost always institutional, as if the questions no longer applied: they go to school, they have jobs—in the candy factory, at the gas station, in a little repair shop, in a diner—and they ride and repair their cars. Many of them live in a moonlight culture, a world where people have second jobs, where mothers work, where one comes home and watches whatever happens to be on television, and where one no longer bothers to flip channels in search of something better.

Some distinctions are easy and obvious. Schooling certifies place; it selects people not only for social class but also for geographic mobility. The college-bound students speak about moving somewhere else—to the cities, to the West Coast, wherever events still permit the fantasy of a better future, or at least of change; the more national the college, the more likely they are to move. Among those who don't go to college there is little talk (except in depressed towns) of moving on. Academic losers stay put. "I know this is a dreary place," said a high school senior in Bethlehem. "But I like dreary places." It wasn't meant to be a joke. Big cities, they tell you again and again, are dangerous. (And in the cities they talk about protecting the neighborhood, or about how *they* still live in a good neighborhood.) Some places, they say, you can't walk the streets without getting knifed—by you know who. You hear it from sixteen-year-olds.

The instrument of oppression is the book. It is still the embodiment of the Great Mystery; learn to understand its secrets and great things will follow. Submit to your instinctive and natural boredom (lacking either the skills to play the game or the security to revolt), and we will use it to persuade you of your benighted incompetence: "I didn't want to write a term paper but the teacher said it would be good if I did; when I handed it in she made fun of it, so I quit school." The family knows that you should stay in school, that you should go to college and "get an education," but it does not know that often the school doesn't work, or that it works principally at the expense of its own kids.

One of the tragedies of the black revolt is that it frequently confused the general incompetence and boorishness of schools with racism, thus helping to persuade much of the blue-collar community that its children were in fine shape, that the educational system was basically sound, and that complaints came either from effete intellectuals or ungrateful, shiftless blacks. Teachers who purported to represent genuine intellectual achievement were thus allowed to continue to conceal their contempt for both kids and brains behind their unwavering passion for conformity and order, and to reaffirm the idea, already favored among working-class parents, that schooling was tough, boring, vicious, and mindless.

The school is an extension of home: in the suburbs it is

rated on college admissions, on National Merit winners, and similar distinctions; in the working-class neighborhood of the city it tends to be judged on order and discipline. Either way, the more talk there was nationally about the need for technologically trained people, the more the school was able to resist challenges to its own authority. "Technological complexity" replaced naked authority as the club of conformity in the school.

What the school did (and is doing) was to sell its clients, young and old, on the legitimacy of the system which abused them. Of course there are exceptions—students, teachers, schools—and even the drearier institutions are sufficiently equipped with the paraphernalia of *fun*—sports, bands, clubs—to mitigate the severity and enlist community support. It is hard to find schools which do not arrogate to themselves some sort of distinction: the state-championship marching band, league leadership in football or track, a squad of belles who twirl, hop, bounce, or step better than any other in the county. A girl makes her way from junior pom-pom girl to cheerleader or majorette, a boy comes from the obscurity of an ethnic neighborhood to be chosen an all-state tackle. There is vitality and engagement and, for the moment, the welding of new common-interest groups, new friendships, new forms of integration. It is the only community adolescents have, and even the dropouts sometimes sneak back to see their friends. And yet, many of these things come to a swift and brutal end: a note in the yearbook, some clippings, a temporary sense of value and distinction convertible into an early marriage, a secretarial job, an occasional scholarship, or into permanent fat. The most prestigious activities of high school have no lasting value; next year, or the year after that, there will be no band, no football, no pep club. Too often, life reaches its highest point at seventeen.

It may well be that even white working-class parents are becoming more suspicious of the mediocrity of their schools, more aware of their crimes, and less taken by the joys they offer. The imperious contempt of large-city administrators is not limited to the complaints of the black community, and the increasing number of defeated school-bond issues and tax overrides is hardly a sign of growing confidence in the school people who proposed them. And yet, the things that have been preached by the best people for a hundred years (and which many of them no longer believe)—order, hard work, self-denial, and the general legitimacy of schooling—these things die hard, or die not at all.

It is too easy to forget the faces, too hard to forget the crowd. American youth, Edgar Friedenberg wrote, are "already deeply implicated in the deeds and values of their culture . . . They go along with it and sincerely believe that in doing so they are putting down troublemakers and serving the best interests of their community." That was, of course, before Berkeley and Columbia, before revolt had reached sufficient mass to be called a "counter-culture." For the children of Mechanic Street, however, nothing changed, except that it added yet another demon to the many others that could not be faced. The kids of the lower middle in the order of the school had always known that they don't have much to say about anything; they have been put down most of their lives by parents, contemptuous teachers, and by fellow students. (The blue collar is still stigmatized; in the school the vocational students are fender-benders, and occasionally a particularly nasty remark is answered with sudden, explosive violence: "He called us grease monkeys, so we pushed him right through that glass door. We stick up for our rights.") What they do have to say is often directed against the most threatening invitations to independence and the most obvious examples of that freedom which constitutes the secret dream. They, most of them, would not permit demonstrations against the Vietnam war, would prefer that their teachers maintain the very order that puts them down, are resentful of anyone that can be called a hippie. ("It's not the parents that cause that," said a student radical. "It's the school. It teaches people to be uptight.") If the war continues at the present rate, several in each of their high school classes will be dead before they ever have a chance to live; of course they would rather not have the war, and a few have joined peace marches and demonstrations, but, they tell you (in the tones of a text they wish they could remember with more confidence—a lesson badly learned and now to be regurgitated on demand) that we have to Resist Communism, have to stand up for our rights. What about My Lai, what about the massacre of women and children in Vietnam? Most of them aren't much disturbed, haven't thought about it, and haven't discussed it or been asked about it. You hear about someone's cousin or brother over in "Nam" who talked about how those crazy people even had kids throwing grenades at our convoys. It's war, and you never know who's going to try and kill you. (They also remind you, of course, that our troops are *their* relatives, and that it's the gooks, not Nixon or Johnson, who are putting their lives in danger.) But the agony of the reply, the painful speech, in class after class, makes it impossible to press too many questions; the Hard Line plays back no better than a Shakespearean sonnet or a Euclidean theorem never worth learning. You do what you're told.

Propaganda and schooling are the same thing. You ought not, you tell yourself, pick on kids.

There is no place to go. No place now, no place ever. For the lower half of the school population—the general course, the voc-ed course, the yet-to-be-certified losers with their low-C grades—the high school is like a refugee camp, a camp for displaced persons waiting for something to happen. The central fact of existence is not school or home or the great institutions of American rhetoric, but the automobile, the one place where life can proceed apart from those institutions, the one place where the stunted remains of the dream of freedom can grow. We have heard all this many times before, have heard about the drag racers, the hot rods, sometimes in amusement, sometimes in indignation, but we haven't come close to understanding how much it means. The car, quite simply, is everything. It is the only place where adult experimentation is tolerated: experiments with sex, with self-realization, with independence, with courage, with change, with death. The car shuttles within the city limits, sometimes to McDonald's or the Burger King, sometimes to the drive-in movie (Clint Eastwood, John Wayne, *Easy Rider*), but rarely beyond, rarely even to the next town.

There is no place to go, except to the car itself. The radio, and the heater, thus become essential accessories, and parking becomes an all-purpose word for sex. It is the thing you do on a date. For the affluent, who have large houses and some privacy—and parental tolerance—to entertain, it may also be an invitation to turn on: sex at home, pot in the car. For those who are not rich, the car represents almost every level of reality: it is something you work on, something useful (or superpowered) that you maintain, it is a place to live, it is escape, it is privacy. If cars are a substitute for sex, car talk is a surrogate for sex talk.

It is hard to get through high school without at least one accident, perhaps even harder to become a man without being able to claim one close call—out on the spur route, or in the empty parking lot of a shopping center late on a Saturday night, someone pulls alongside, you give the engine everything, and for a few brief moments you feel speed and power and triumph. People don't grow up with cars; they grow up in them.

There is much talk, in town after town, about having places for "young people to go," about teen centers and recreation halls (the chaperoned dances having been abandoned by all but junior high students), but that concern seems to reflect a deeper despair about the community, about *place*, and about the future itself. As the old ethnic and regional culture breaks up, the culture of aspiration—what we used to call the mainstream—should grow in its power to attract and hold, but often, needless to say, it does not. In the smaller towns and in the hyphenated neighborhoods of cities, traditional patterns and institutions—food, family, the church, the Ukrainian Hall, the Polish-American Club—become increasingly tenuous; church membership grows older, the neighborhood more bland, the swimming hole more distant, the culture more thin. The local mill, the mine, or the plant, once ferocious and mythic in its demands on men, in its economic unpredictability, in its brutality, is tamed by unions, by government, and by corporate management itself. The kids don't remember the last strike, the last layoffs, let alone the last fight with the Pinkertons, the National Guard and the company dicks. In the cities—in Astoria or South Boston, or on the North Side of Chicago —the kids may still hang out at the corner, or the local Coke-and-juke joint, sending their quarters and dimes after the Fifth Dimension or Blood, Sweat and Tears, jiving the girls, and in the small towns they still learn to hunt and fish ("They just love to get a gun under their arm," said a teacher with a gesture that indicated more about impotence than woodsmanship), and they still go to the basketball games on Friday night. There may be nothing more democratic or joyful than the crowd at a high school game in a small Northern city. But every year a few more landmarks disappear, another memory dies, another set of roots is destroyed.

For most parents, there is still the hope of a better place, and almost every one of them does his best to get his kid to go. But the ebullient romance, the Alger myths, the dream of adventure and enterprise—all those things have been inundated by size and technology, and abandoned by the very people who invented them in the first place. The fact that things are less manageable, that the country and the world no longer respond the way we once imagined they should (or that they have become unmanageable altogether) may not be as traumatic for the ethnic and social underclass which had never controlled much of anything anyway, but it does reduce the interest and the fun of trying to join. One of the striking things is that many kids are not ambitious for power or possessions. "My parents," said one, "never had what they wanted; they couldn't get along on what they had. But we can." And yet the life that he and many others imagine is almost identical to the life of the present. As today opens up a little—a better home, a car, a television set and a steady job—tomorrow seems to close down. Modesty in achievement and ambition is matched by an inability to visualize anything substantially richer, in experience or possessions, or in the world at large. The generation gap—

for rich, for poor, for all—is precisely this: that many kids, for the first time, are growing up without a sense of the future. And that, for America, is new.

They sit in those refugee camps, people who have lost one country and haven't yet found another. Some of them are at least marginal participants in the "counter-culture"; the hair on the boys grows longer, the hard rock is universal, and drugs (pot and pills), now prevalent among the swingers (college prep, affluent, or black), are beginning to infiltrate the middle, often with the tacit acquiescence of the cops, who know that they have lost some of their most troublesome adolescent clients to the euphoria of pot, and who are, in any case, powerless to stop it. There may still be high schools in America where drugs aren't traded, but they are probably scarcer than dry towns. (Narcotics would, of course, be a great accessory to any police state; they make political enemies vulnerable "under the law" and reduce the general will to resist). At the same time, the potential for revolt, for repression, for violence, random and directed, remains. In one high school, a senior—long hair, mustache, articulate—speaks about his plans: when he graduates he will join the Marine Corps, get to Vietnam "where the action is," then return home and become a state cop. "I'll cut my hair before *they* get to it," trading one form of expression for another. Perhaps there are few alternatives left. Perhaps Vietnam remains one of the viable ways to become a man, or to become anything at all.

"Maybe," said a sophisticated high school teacher, "we'd better leave everything alone. If these kids ever become politically conscious, who knows whether they'll join the SDS or the brownshirts." There are signs that they could do either, just like anyone else. Some of them have harassed peace demonstrators, heckled civil rights marchers and have beaten up black kids in integrated schools or on the periphery of changing neighborhoods, and have been beaten up in return. And while middle-class, college-oriented students, and blacks, have made the papers with their activism, there have also been, in some of the inner cities, self-styled proto-fascist gangs hunting blacks, hippies, and other signs of vulnerable liberalism. In the 1968 election the major support for George Wallace within the labor movement came from younger members, the older brothers of the kids now finishing school. At the same time it is also the young union members who are most likely to challenge the adequacy of negotiated contracts, to start wildcat strikes, and to question their labor leadership in general. They do not have a historic fear of unemployment, of long strikes and hard times, and they have learned enough (perhaps from their college contemporaries) about challenging authority to make themselves heard. If college students have lacked the cooling discipline of economic insecurity, so, to a lesser extent, has everyone else. (It is almost impossible, however, to overestimate the effect of the credit system on labor-management relations: people who are overmortgaged and over their heads in installment payments aren't likely to vote for a casual strike, and management knows it.)

Who is to say how things are ever learned? For the children of Mechanic Street, as for all others, the classroom has never been more than a marginal place. Except for minimal literacy and a few tricks picked up in a home-ec course, the girl who marries at eighteen was educated at home, though she may well have used the school to find her husband. Except for that certification which schools bestow on good behavior and acceptable habits, the boy who takes a job immediately after graduation (or who, with a fifth of his peers, never graduated at all) takes little from his school, except perhaps a vaguely inexpressible sense of defeat.

And yet, something is learned—perhaps from television, perhaps from the school community itself. The well-publicized tension between generations seems to have given language and content to the specific tensions between all parents and children. Which is to say that "student revolt" or "youth revolt" seems to be applicable even where there are no students and no "youth" who identify with larger causes; in other words, the threat of protests and demonstrations is not so much political as it is personal. It hits people where they live. (Or, conversely, it threatens to politicize the family.) There are few political radicals among blue-collar families (Are there genuine radicals anywhere?), and yet even politically conservative and/or apathetic kids now seem to be able—or even compelled, under pressure to get with it—to articulate differences with their parents. Many of them revolve around nothing newer than the company they keep, the people they date, and the time they have to be home at night. Nonetheless, the atmosphere of revolt provides new strategies for all (long hair, for example), opens new possibilities and offers new ways of rationalizing old ones. "I'm doing my thing," said the daughter of Russian immigrants. And what is that? "I'm going to college and then I'm going to be a schoolteacher." Do her parents object? No, they seem to approve, but still she's doing her thing.

Marshall McLuhan's notion of the global village may still be more vanity than reality, yet it is accurate in one major respect: the media—television, radio and records—are creating communities where none existed before. If SDS has failed in its attempts to politicize or organize factory workers, the media are creating bonds of style, age, and interest that transcend the particularities of locality and background. The surface manifestations of a style may themselves satisfy the longing for place and identity, providing alternatives for the local and immediate places (neighborhoods, rituals, traditions) that no longer exist. In this sense, "revolt" is the opiate of the masses. High school reform and protest may never go beyond the abandonment of the dress code. But the media may also be creating the possibilities both for the development of new forms of consciousness and culture and (for the same reason) centralized political management and control. Unless Americans are prepared to revolutionize their educational system by providing far more intellectual and cultural freedom and diversity than they are currently willing to allow, the high school will, in fact, be no more than a huge amplifier for the signals that the media are willing (or permitted) to transmit. Considering the unbelievable boredom and crudeness of the slow track (or the "general course," by whatever name) in the average high school, and the treatment accorded its students, no "educator" can berate TV without being laughed off the stage. If there is any escape from that crudeness, it is in the car and in television itself. The children are moving away from Mechanic Street. But where will they go?

WHAT HAPPENED TO MAIN STREET?

MASON CITY, IOWA. Pop. 32,642. Meat packing, Portland cement, brick and tile, beet sugar, dairy products, commercial feeds, soybean oil and meal, thermopane windows and mobile homes. At the intersection of Highways 18 and 65, 135 miles south of Minneapolis, 125 miles north of Des Moines. Three major railroads. Ozark Airlines. Daily newspaper, one local television station. Library, art museum.

Among the most difficult things in any small American town is to stay more than a few days and remain an outsider. There seems to be a common feeling that anyone—even a writer from New York—is, somewhere in his heart, a small-town boy come home. The light but unceasing stream of traffic which moves through Main Street—Federal Avenue in Mason City—north to Minneapolis and beyond, south to Des Moines, reinforces the belief that this flat, open place is part of a great American continuity extending through other Main Streets, across the fields of corn and beets, past tractor depots and filling stations, past grain elevators and loading pens to the very limits of the national imagination. It must make it difficult to conceive of anyone as a total stranger, for being here—local pride notwithstanding—cannot seem very different from being anywhere else.

They take you in, absorb you, soak you up; they know whom you've seen, where you've been, what you've done. In Mississippi hamlets the sheriff follows you around; here it is The Word. *Small towns co-opt (you tell yourself) and nice small towns co-opt absolutely.* But it is not just them, it's you. The things that you bring with you—your sense of yourself as a friendly sort, the wish to believe that the claims of small-town virtue are valid, and your particular kind of chauvinism—all these make you a willing collaborator. So maybe they're right. *Maybe we're all just small-town boys come home.* Yes, you're willing to come to dinner, to visit the Club, to suspend the suspicion that all this is some sort of do-it-yourself Chamber of Commerce trick. Later perhaps (says the Inner Voice of Reason) you will be able to sort things out, to distinguish Main Street from the fantasies that you and a lot of other people from New York have invented for it. Later.

You have come here to see what is happening to the heart of this country, to ask how the great flat democracy responds to Vietnam and Black Power, to marijuana and Mark Rudd, to see how it is taking technology and the

Bomb—all the things that overwhelm the visible spectrum of public concern. Is there something here that can survive in New York and Chicago, is there an Americanism that will endure, or will it perish with the farm and the small town? What, you ask, is happening to Main Street? Later. For the moment you are simply in it, listening to them worry about a proposed civic center, about the construction of a mall, about taxes and industrial development, and about something called "the traffic problem" which, by even the more placid standards of New York, seems more imagined than real.

There are ghosts in this country—local ghosts, and ghosts that you bring with you, that refuse to stay behind: shades of brawling railroad workers and dispossessed farmers; frontiersmen and Babbitts; the old remembered tales of reaction and America First, of capital *R* Republicanism and the Ku Klux Klan; the romance of Jefferson and Frederick Jackson Turner, the yeoman farmer and the self-made man. As a place of literary irony, Middle America is celebrating its golden anniversary. "Main Street," wrote Sinclair Lewis in 1920, "is the climax of civilization. That this Ford car might stand in front of the Bon Ton Store, Hannibal invaded Rome and Erasmus wrote in Oxford cloisters. What Ole Jensen the grocer says to Ezra Stowbody the banker is the new law for London, Prague and the unprofitable isles of the sea; whatsoever Ezra does not know and sanction, that thing is heresy, worthless for knowing and wicked to consider." But that irony, too, may be a ghost—now as much myth, perhaps, as the self-flattering cultural propositions invented to answer it. ("Right here in Mason City," someone tells you, "we sell three hundred tickets each year for the Metropolitan Opera tour performances in Minneapolis.") The life of Babbittry, you tell yourself, follows the life (and art) of others.

But the models are no longer clear. Main Street once insisted on rising from Perfection (rural) to Progress (urban): Sauk Centre and Zenith were trying to do Chicago's Thing, but what does Chicago have to offer now? The Main Street boosters are still there, hanging signs across the road proclaiming "A Community on the March," but their days are numbered. How would Lewis have portrayed the three hundred marchers of the Vietnam moratorium in Mason City? How would he deal with the growing number of long-haired pot-smoking kids? Here, too, Mason City follows New York and Chicago (The Mafia, you are told, controls the floating dice games that occasionally rumble through the back rooms of a local saloon.) The certainty of Lewis's kind of irony was directed to the provincial insularity that war, technology, and television are rendering obsolete. Main Street lives modern not in its dishwashers and combines—not even in Huntley-Brinkley and Walter Cronkite—but in its growing ambivalence about the America that creates them, the America that crosses the seas of beets and corn—and therefore about itself.

It is not a simple place, and perhaps never was. You see what you expect, and then begin to see (or imagine) what you did not. Standard America, yes: the Civil War monument in the Square; the First National Bank; Osco's Self-Service Drugs; the shoe store and movie theaters; Damon's and Younkers' ("Satisfaction Always"); Maizes's and Penney's; Sears and Monkey Ward. Middle America the way it was supposed to be; the farmers come to shop on Saturday afternoon; the hunting and fishing; the high school football game Friday night; the swimming and sailing at Clear Lake, a small resort nine miles to the west. You cannot pass through town without being told that Mason City is a good place to raise a family, without

hearing praise for the schools, and without incessant reminders that Meredith Willson's musical play *The Music
Man* was *about* Mason City, that Willson was born here,
and that the town was almost renamed River City because of it. (There *is* a river, the Winnebago, which makes
itself known only at times of flood.) Mr. Toot, the figure of
a trombone-blowing bandsman (says a man at the Chamber of Commerce), is now the town symbol. "We hope,"
says the man, "that we can make our band festival into a
major event." Someday, you imagine, this could be the
band capital of the nation, and maybe the whole wicked
universe.

Mason City, they tell you, is a stable community: steady
population, little unemployment, no race problem (there
are, at most, 300 Negroes in town), clean water and, with
some huffy qualifications (dust from one of the cement
plants, odor from the packing house) clean air. A cliché.
In the *Globe Gazette*, the editor, Bob Spiegel, suggests
that the problems and resources of the large cities be
dispersed to all the Mason Cities in America. A Jeffersonian, Mr. Spiegel, and a nice guy: "The smaller communities need the plants and the people that are polluting the urban centers—not in large doses, but steadily,
surely . . . The small communities are geared up. They
have comprehensive plans. They know they can't stand
still or they will be passed by." Stable, perhaps, but what
is stable in a relativistic universe? The very thing that
Spiegel proposes seems to be happening in reverse. The
community is becoming less pluralistic: it has fewer Negroes, fewer Jews, and fewer members of other minorities
than it had twenty years ago. "After the war," said Nate
Levinson, an attorney, who is president of the synagogue,
"we had eighty Jewish families. Now we have forty. We
can't afford a rabbi any more." On the few occasions that

Mason City has tried to attract Negro professionals, they refused to come or to stay. There is nobody to keep them company, and the subtle forms of discrimination—in housing and employment—are pervasive enough to discourage pioneers. ("My maid says if she hears any more about Black Power she'll scream . . . I wouldn't mind one living next door, if he mowed the grass and kept the place neat.") The brighter kids—black and white—move away, off to college, off to the cities, and beneath that migration one can sense the fear that the city's declining agricultural base will not be replaced by enough industrial jobs to maintain even the stability which now exists.

Mason City is not a depressed town, although in its stagnating downtown shopping area it often looks like one. (Shopping centers are thriving on the periphery: the farmers come in to shop, but not all the way.) The city shares many of the attributes of other small Middle Western communities, competing with them for industry, counting, each week, another farm family which is selling out or giving up, counting the abandoned houses around the county, counting the number of acres (now exceeding two hundred) required for efficient agricultural operation. An acre of land costs $500, a four-row combine $24,000. If you stop in places like Plymouth, a town of 400, nine miles from Mason City, you hear the cadences of compromise and decline: men who have become part-time farmers who make ends meet, at $2.25 an hour, by working in the sugar mill in Mason City. Independence becomes, ever more, a hopeful illusion belied by abandoned shops and boarded windows, and by tales of success set in other places: an engineer in California, a chemist in Detroit, a teacher in Oregon.

Iowa, you realize, not just from statistics, but from faces, is a state of old people: "What do the kids here want to do? What do the kids in Mason City want to do? What do the kids in Iowa want to do? They want to get out. I'd get out, go to California if I could." There is a double migration, from farms into towns, from the towns into the cities, and out of state. More than 10 percent of Mason City's work force is employed at the Decker Packing Plant on the north side of town. (The plant is a division of Armour and Co.) At the moment the plant is prosperous; it pays good wages. (A hamboner—who does piece work—can make $6 to $7 an hour.) But what would happen, said one of the city's corporate managers, if the place should succumb to the increasing efficiency of smaller plants? "What'll we do the day—and don't quote me—when the place has to shut down?"

It is the fashion to worry slow, worry with a drawl. Urgency and crisis are not the style. Through most of its history, Mason City was dominated by a few families, and to some extent it still is, not because they are so powerful, but because Federal Avenue once thought they were. Small towns create their own patriarchs, tall men who look even taller against the flatness of history, producing, inevitably, a belief that civic motion and inertia are the subtle work of Big Men—bankers, real estate operators and corporate managers. Mason City still talks about the General, Hanford MacNider (banking, cement, real estate) who was an assistant secretary of war under Coolidge, ambassador to Canada, an aspirant for the 1940 Republican nomination for president, and, for a time, a supporter of America First. (In Mason City, MacNider was *Secretary* of War and barely missed becoming president). The MacNiders gave the city land for parks, for the public library and for a museum. (The General was also a founder of the Euchre and Cycle Club, a lunch-and-dinner club—all the best people—which still has no Jewish members, and he is remembered, among other things, as the man who did not lower his flag for thirty days after John F. Kennedy was killed.) "My father," said Jack MacNider, now president of the Northwestern States Portland Cement Co., "was quite a guy. Some people thought he was tough. To some he was a patron saint. You should have known him."

The General's shadow survived him, and there are still people who are persuaded that nothing of major consequence can be accomplished in Mason City against the opposition of the family. Is that true, you ask Jack, sitting in his second-story office overlooking Federal Avenue. (There is a picture of the General, in full uniform, behind Jack's desk). "I'm flattered," he answers, not defensively, but with some amusement, saying more between the lines than on the record, telling you—you imagine—that the MacNiders take the rap for a lot of small-town inertia they can't control, and that they suffer (or enjoy) a visibility for which they haven't asked. At this very moment a young lawyer named Tom Jolas, a second-generation Greek, is challenging the Establishment (such as it is) in his campaign for mayor; you both know that Jolas is likely to win (on November 4 he did win, handily) and that the city's style and mood is now determined as much by younger businessmen and professionals—and by hundreds of packing-house workers and cement workers—as it is by the old families. "This must be a fishbowl for the Mac-Niders," you say, and Jack offers no argument. And when you speak about prejudice in Mason City, Jack agrees—yes, there is—but you can't be sure whether he means against Catholics, Jews and Negroes (or Greeks and Chicanos) or also against the MacNiders. The shadow is still there, but the General is dead.

Mason City's traditional style of politics and political

behavior was nicely represented by sixty-five-year-old George Mendon, who was mayor for sixteen years until Jolas beat him. Small towns always create the illusion of responsiveness—you can call any public official, any corporate manager, with little interference from secretaries who ask your business, your name, and your pedigree—and you thus can walk into Mendon's office unannounced and receive an audience. But you are never sure that, once in, you have really arrived anywhere. The action must be someplace else. The room is almost bare, the desk virtually clean, the man without visible passion. Yes, jobs and industrial development are a problem, and Mason City has done pretty well, but there are twenty thousand other towns trying to attract industry and, you know, these things take time. Yes, they would like to hire some Negoes for the police force, but none have been qualified. Yes, the MacNiders had been good to the city—all that land they'd given (and all those tax deductions?) but . . . When Mendon was challenged during the campaign about operating an underpaid and undertrained police force, he answered that the city had the most modern equipment, including riot guns, mace, and bulletproof vests. What are they for, you ask, and Mendon, rattling the change in his pocket, identifies himself. "Our colored population is peaceful," he said. "They wouldn't riot. But you never know when people from the outside might come in and try to start something." Mason City is prepared for Watts and Newark, and somewhere in its open heart there lurks an edge of apprehension that the fire next time might burn even here. But when Mendon spoke about his riot guns at an open meeting, the general response was tempered by considerable facetious amusement, and the people who were amused went out to vote against him, and beat him.

There is no single current running against the old style

of politics, or against the Mendons and the Establishment they are supposed to represent. In 1968 Mason City voted for Nixon, for the conservative Congressman H. R. Gross, and for Harold Hughes, a liberal Democrat. ("We helped elect Gross the first time he ran," said a union official, "and we've been sorry ever since.") Sociology and political calculations don't help much. "The issue here," said Bud Stewart, who runs a music store and worked for Jolas, "is generational," implying that whatever was young and progressive supported the challenger against the older Establishment. Jolas campaigned under the slogan "Time for a Change," including, among other things, concern for public housing (which the city does not have but desperately needs), more attention to the problems of youth, and the creation of a modern police force that could meet what he called the rising rate of crime. (And which meant, I was told, getting rid of the reactionary police chief who had bought all the riot junk.) But what Jolas said was clearly not as important as what he is: young, energetic and, beneath it all, ambiguously liberal and unambiguously decent. "I had my hair long and wore sideburns," he tells you (two years ago, he managed a teen-age rock band), "but my friends said I couldn't win with it, so I cut it short. But maybe after the election I might get a notion and let it grow again."

Jolas's great political achievement before he ran for mayor was to force the State to re-route a projected interstate highway so that it would pass within a few miles of Mason City, but it was undoubtedly personality rather than politics that elected him. ("You know what they're saying about me," he mused one day toward the end of the campaign. "They're saying that if I'm elected the Greeks and the niggers are going to take over Mason City. I even had someone charge that I belong to the

Mafia, the Greek Mafia.") More than anything else, Jolas seems to have a sense of concern about youth—not a program but an awakening awareness of how kids are shortchanged by schools, politicians, by adults. ("He knows," I write in my notes, "that the world screws kids.")

What Jolas can achieve is doubtful. He will not have a sympathetic city council, or perhaps even a sympathetic community, and his commitment to a downtown Civic Center and mall as a means of restoring the vitality of the central business area may be more the tokens of modernism than the substance of progress, yet it is clear that Jolas received the support, and represented the aspirations of whatever liberalism (black, labor, professional) that the city could muster. If you sit in his storefront headquarters long enough you learn how far Main Street has come from Babbittry. You meet Mary Dresser, the recently widowed wife of a lawyer who, as president of the Iowa League of Women Voters, carried a reapportionment fight through the legislature and who speaks of how, when their son decided to grow a mustache, she and her husband decided to back him up against the school authorities and how, eventually, they won; Jean Beatty, the wife of a psychologist, answering phone calls and stuffing Jolas envelopes, and shuttling between meetings of the League and the local branch of the NAACP, knowing that the organization should be run by black people but knowing also that its precariously weak membership cannot sustain it without help; or Jim Shannon, the County Democratic chairman, who has worked for the Milwaukee Railroad all his life and who has gone back to the local community college (working nights, studying economics during the day), speaking in his soft, laconic, infinitely American cadences about the campaign for Bobby Kennedy in 1968, about a decade of legislative fights, reminding you, without meaning to or even mentioning it, that liberalism wasn't invented in New York, that the Phil Harts, the Frank Churches, the Fred Harrises and the George McGoverns weren't elected by professors.

If that were all—if one could merely say that Mason City and Middle America are going modern—it would all be easy, but they are not. (What, after all, is modern, uniquely modern, after you've dispensed with the technology?) The national culture is there, mass cult, high, middle and low, mod and trad: Bud Stewart in the Edwardian double-breasted suits which he orders from advertisements through the local stores; the elite trooping off to Minneapolis to hear the Met when it comes on tour, or to Ames to catch the New York Philharmonic (mostly, say the cynics, to be conspicuous, not for love of music); the rock on the radio and in the jukes (The Fifth Dimension, Blood, Sweat and Tears, new Dylan and old Baez, plus some leavening from the likes of Johnny Cash); the long hair and the short skirts, the drugs and the booze. (At the same time, beer, rather than pot, seems still to be the preponderant, though not the exclusive, form of adolescent sin.) But somehow what Mason City receives through the box and the tube, and from its trips to Minneapolis and Des Moines, where some of the ladies do almost weekly shopping, it seems to shape and reshape into its own forms. There is a tendency to mute the decibels of public controversy and social friction, perhaps because people are more tolerant and relaxed, perhaps because they are simply less crowded. There is talk about crime and violence, but the most common local examples seem usually to involve the theft of bicycles and the destruction of Halloween pumpkins. (Another way of staking a claim on the modern?) If you ask long enough, you can get some of the blue-collar workers to speak about

their resentment against welfare, taxes, and student demonstrators (not at Harvard, mind you, but at the State
University of Iowa), but it is commonly only television
and the newspapers that produce the talk—and so it tends
to be dispassionate, distant, and somewhat abstract.
Bumper stickers and decals are scarce; you rarely see
American flags on the rear windows of automobiles because, one might assume, there aren't many people at
whom to wave them, not many devils to exorcise. The
silent majority here is an abstraction, a collage of minorities, except when it comes to the normalcy of the ladies'
study clubs and bridge clubs, the football, the hunting and
fishing, and the trip to the lake. And every two years they
go back, most of them, and vote for H. R. Gross.

And yet, here are the kids, high school students and students at the Community College, organizing a moratorium
march, running a little newspaper, semi-underground
within the high school, and with the blessing of the school
authorities; here are the clergymen, not all, but a few,
giving their support for the march from the pulpit (when
she heard her minister that Sunday, one prominent parish-
ioner promptly resigned from the church); and here are
ordinary people responding to the critics of dissent with
their own protest. In a letter to the *Globe Gazette:*

> We supported the Moratorium Day demonstration. We
> have a son in Vietnam. We love our country. We fly the
> American flag.
>
> But we do not believe in blindly following our leader
> as the Germans did when their leader decided to exter-
> minate the Jews or as some Americans would do if our
> leader should decide to exterminate the Indians.
>
> We feel our country was wrong to send 40,000 of our
> boys to their death, not defending their own shores.

> Supporting the Moratorium was our way of saying we
> love our country right or wrong, and this time it was
> wrong.

Given the reputation of the average small town in
America, the greatest surprise is the school system which,
under Rod Bickert, the superintendent, and John Pattswald, the high school principal, has managed to move well
beyond the expected, even in the conventional modern
suburb. Mason City has abandoned dress codes in its high
school, has instituted flexible-modular scheduling (meaning that students have only a limited number of formal
lecture classes, and can do their own thing—in "skill" and
study centers, in the library or the cafeteria—as they will)
and has begun to experiment, in the high school, with an
"open mike" where any student can talk to the entire
school on anything he pleases. There are no bells, no
monitors. As you walk through the halls (modern, sprawl-
ing, corporate style), Pattswald, a Minnesotan, explains
that he first came to the school as a disciplinarian. "It was
a conservative school and I ran a tight ship." When he
became principal he turned things around. "We're something of an island, and when some of the parents first
heard about it they thought it was chaos. We had an open
meeting—parents and students—to explain the flex-mod
schedule, but most of the parents wanted to know about
dress. (You know, we have everything here, including
girls in miniskirts and pants suits.) The students helped us
carry it. They know that some sort of uproar could blow
this thing right out of the water, but I think they can do
the job."

Every day Pattswald spends a couple of hours visiting
classes, asking students irreverent questions that are, at
least tangentially, directed to the teachers. "I ask them

why they're doing what they're doing; what's the significance of this, why study it at all? Sure, we have some
weak teachers, but now when I hire people I role-play
with them a little, I want to see how they take pressure.
In the classroom it's too easy for the teachers always to
be the last resort and to put the screws down. That's no
way to improve the climate of learning." The conversation
is frequently interrupted while Pattswald stops to talk
with students (he knows many by name), and later to tell
you about them. "Kids are my life," he says, rounding a
corner after a brief encounter with two boys. "The whole
point is to get them to appreciate the worth of an individual. We have to reach the ones who are overlooked, like
one boy they were taunting and who talked about himself as 'a ball that they always kick around.' Those are the
ones we have to reach. But I think we're coming."

The militant students seek you out. Mason City is still
a confining place, and they find the visitor from New
York, the outsider, walking through the hall alone: the
organizers of the moratorium, the editors of the mimeo-
graphed paper, the *Bitter End* (not quite underground,
not quite official), the activists, sons and daughters of the
affluent lawyers and doctors, all local people, not carpet-
baggers from the East. The school, they say, is
divided between "pointy heads like us" and "the animals."
(A group passes through the hall after school and the
pointy heads, through a glass door, follow the herd with
"Moo-moo," "Oink-oink.") The radicals still see the school
as a fraud. "There is no way to get a decent education in
a public school. Everybody's too uptight." Like what?
"Like being allowed to leave school during your unstruc-
tured time to make a movie. You can get a release to dish
hamburgers at McDonald's, so why not to make movies?"
One of them gets threatening letters for his part in the

peace movement, another loses his allowance because he won't cut his hair. Their lives are no different, nor are their parents', from those of similar people in Scarsdale or Shaker Heights or Winnetka. (Some of them, said Pattswald, "have told their parents to go to hell.") What is surprising is that, although they are a lonely minority, they are in Mason City (bands, football, cheerleaders, Toot)—that they are in this community at all.

For the majority of the young, the concerns are universal: cars, dances, sports. You hear them in Vic's ("Real Dago Pizza"): "It's a '65 Chevvy. I traded it for that car that was sitting in the grass by the Hub . . . paid three hundred and fifty dollars and put a new engine in it and it runs great." They want to go to college, to get jobs—more than half the high school students work—so they can maintain those automobiles, get married. The modest dream is to become an airline stewardess; "if I'm not too clumsy," to enlist in the Army; to learn a trade. On Friday nights they cruise up and down Federal, shuttling from a root-beer stand at the south end to a drive-in at the other. There is some talk about establishing a teen center, a place Where Kids Can Go, but the proposal draws little enthusiasm from adults and less from the kids. And yet, even among the majority—the animals, the apathetic—something may be happening. The war perhaps, or television, or the music. There was a time, said a school administrator, "when the war seemed very distant." Mason City's enlistment rate was always high, the college students were exempt anyway, and the draft wasn't much of an issue. But in the past year eight recent graduates of Mason City High were killed in Vietnam, making death and change more personal. Nearly a hundred turned out to hear discussions about the war inside the school, and while the patriotic speakers still come to address the assembly, other messages are being heard as well. The hair gets longer, the music a little harder, and the news is on everybody's set.

The young are slowly becoming mediators of the culture, they receive the signals from the outside and interpret the messages for adults. And that's new for all America, not just for Mason City. "The kids are having an effect on their parents," said a mental-health worker, one of the few clinicians in town, apparently, that the adolescents are willing to trust. "People here are friendly and uptight at the same time. Many of them take the attitude that the children should have their fun, that eventually they'll come around to their parents' view. But people have been jarred—by TV and by their own children, and they know, some of them at least, that they've got to listen. They're trying to become looser."

But becoming looser is still a struggle and, given the conditions of life, an imperative that can be deferred. ("I'm *not* going to send my son to Harvard," says a Harvard graduate. "An eighteen-year-old is not mature enough to handle SDS and all that other garbage.") The space, the land, the weather, the incessant reminders of physical normalcy make it possible to defer almost anything. Church on Sunday, football on Friday and the cycle of parties, dinners, and cookouts remain more visible (not to say comprehensible) than the subtleties of cultural change or social injustice. If the churches and their ministers are losing some of their influence among the young (and if the call for psychiatrists is increasing), they are still holding their members, and if the Catholic Monsignor, Arthur Breen, has to schedule a folk mass at Holy Family every Sunday (in addition to four other masses) he nonetheless continues to pack them in.

What you see most of all (see is not a good word—feel, maybe) is a faith in the capacity of people and institutions to be responsive, the belief that, finally, things are pretty much what they seem, that Things Work. "This is just a big farm town," said a Mason City businessman. "You don't check people's credit here; you just assume they'll pay their bills. In Waterloo, which is really an industrial city, even though it isn't very big, you check everybody out." The answer to an economic problem is to work harder, to take a second job, or to send your wife to work, usually as a clerk or a waitress. (Wages for women are extremely low.) On the radio, Junior Achievement makes its peace with modernism by setting its jingle to "Get With It" to a rock beat, but the message of adolescent enterprise (Babbittry?) is the same, and around the lunch tables at the Green Mill Restaurant or the bar at Tom MacNider's Chart House it is difficult to convince anyone that sometimes even people with the normal quota of ambition can't make it.

The advantages of that faith are obvious, but their price is high. "This is a nice town as long as you don't rock the boat," said Willis Haddix, a meat packer who is president of the struggling Mason City chapter of NAACP. "What's wrong here is in the secret places": in subtle discrimination in housing and jobs; in the out-of-sight dilapidated frame houses at the north and south ends of town, buildings surrounded with little piles of old lumber, rusting metal chairs, decaying junk cars once slated for repair; in the lingering aroma of personal defeat; and in the cross between arrogance and apathy that declares "there are no poor people in this area." On Sundays, while most people are packing their campers for the trip home, or making the transition between Church and television football, the old, who have little to do, wander into the Park Inn for lunch (hot roast-beef sandwiches for $1.25), and talk about medicare. And against theirs you hear other voices: Murray Lawson, for example, a civilized, compassionate man who represents Mason City in the legislature, saying, "We've been generous with education, but not so generous with the old; we've had a rough time with nursing homes"; Jim Shannon who supports his wife and seven children on the salary of a railroad clerk and janitor, describing the effects of a regressive sales tax that victimizes the small man but makes little impact on the rich; the official of the local OEO poverty agency talking about the county's third welfare generation and reflecting that "an admission of poverty is an admission of failure, and people here don't do that"; Tom Jolas describing Mason City's enthusiasm for the New York Mets when they won the World Series after a ninth-place finish in 1968 because "people believe in coming off the bottom."

And then you learn something else—about yourself, and about the phenomenon you choose to call Main Street. You hear them complain about Eastern urban provincialism, people who cannot believe that Mason City has television ("You must get it from the West Coast"), let alone an art museum, a decent library, or a couple of go-go joints (or that you can buy Philip Roth, Malcolm X and Henry Miller in the bookstore), and you begin to understand, almost by suggestion, what the barriers of comprehension are all about. Is it really surprising that Main Street cannot fully comprehend talk about police brutality, police rigidity, or social disillusionment? If the system works here, why doesn't it work everywhere else?

Main Street's uniquely provincial vice lies in its excessive, unquestioning belief in the Protestant ethic—hard work, honesty—and conventional politics; New York's in the conviction that most of the time nothing may make much difference, that institutions and public life are by their very nature unresponsive. And if New York has come to doubt the values and the beliefs of tradition, it still hasn't invented anything to replace them. The anger of the blue-collar worker—at welfare, students, Negroes—is rooted in the frustrated ethic of Main Street, frustrated not only in its encounters with urban problems and technology but also in the growing doubt of the Best People —Wallace's pointy heads, Agnew's effete impudent snobs— that it still has merit. Among the characteristic excesses of rural populism (whether expressed by William Jennings Bryan, Joe McCarthy or Spiro Agnew) was a paranoia about Them: the Bankers, the railroads, the Eastern Establishment, the Communists in government. But paranoia is surely also one of the characteristic defenses of almost every other inhabitant of New York. (If you try to explain the vicissitudes of dealing with Con Edison or the New York Telephone Company, most people in Mason City stare at you in disbelief; if you speak about rents and housing they're certain you've gone mad.) Every rural or small-town vote against some proposal for the alleviation of a problem in New York or Chicago or Cleveland is not merely an act of self-interest (keeping taxes low, protecting the farmers) but also a gesture of disbelief that Main Street's ethic and tactics—if they were really applied—would be ineffective in the Big City.

At the end, sitting in the waiting room at the municipal airport (all flights from Chicago are late, naturally), you detach yourself. You hear, still, one of the Federal Avenue lawyers saying, "This town is solid; it's solid as a commercial center and as a medical and cultural center for a

large region." You see his nearly bare office—the brown
wood furniture, the linoleum floors, and the fluorescent
lights—see his partner, in a sleeveless gray pullover, walking through the outer office (Clarence Darrow?), and hear
the trucks stopping for the red light at the intersection
below. You hear Jack MacNider speaking about the
gradual movement of the "iron triangle," the Midwestern
industrial region, into north central Iowa, speaking about
the ultimate industrialization of the area around the city.
You see the high school homecoming queen, fragile and
uncomfortable in the back of an open convertible in the
wind-chilled stadium; see the wide residential streets with
their maples and time-threatened elms, the section of
magnificent houses by Prairie School architects, one of
them by Frank Lloyd Wright, and the crumbling streets
at the south end, near the Brick and Tile, and you hear,
in that same neighborhood, two NAACP ladies, one white,
one Negro, discussing the phrasing of a letter to the school
board politely protesting the use of *Little Black Sambo*
in the elementary grades. And then, finally, you hear again
all those people speaking about how good Mason City is
for raising a family, and you wonder what kind of society
it is that must separate growing up and the rearing of children from the places where most of its business is trans-
acted, its ideas discussed and its policies determined. And
then you wonder, too, what would happen if something
ever came seriously to disturb Main Street's normalcy, if
direct demands were ever made, if the letters ceased
being polite, if the dark places—the discrimination and
disregard—were probed and, for the first time, tested.
Small towns do co-opt, you think, not by what they do,
not by their hospitality, but by what we wish they were—
because all of us, big city boys and small, *want* to believe.
And yet, when Ozark 974 rises from the runway, off to

Dubuque, over the corn and beets, over the Mississippi, off to Chicago, you know that you can't go home again, that the world is elsewhere, and that every moment the distances grow not smaller but greater. Main Street is far away.

[1970]

TENNESSEE'S
LONESOME END

The scene is like a tribal memory, a fantasy of the race. In the last triumphant moments of the afternoon, the rays of the low autumn sun filter through the banners of the Confederacy, softening the colors, and, behind the halo of light and dust, sever the now-faceless crowd from the immediacy of place and moment. Can they hear the cheers in Tupelo, can they feel the cadences in Clarksdale and Meridian and Biloxi? *Mississippi 21, Tennessee Nothing; Mississippi 24, Tennessee Nothing; Mississippi 31, Tennessee Nothing; Missis-*

sippi 38, Tennessee Nothing. "Rebs Put Big Squeeze on
Big Orange 38-0." The intensity, hysterical, catatonic, is of
the moment, but the currents that give it life are beyond
football, beyond place and time, flowing from some underground source which rises here. At the end of the game
the shades of Horace Benbow and Temple Drake—Faulk-
nerian ghosts in camel's hair coats and bouffant wigs—will
wander across the field, greeting other ghosts, replaying the
game through the exits, through the parking lots, through
the lobbies of Howard Johnson Motels and Holiday Inns,
through bars and country clubs, far into the evening and
through the night, shouting "To hell with Tennessee,"
"To hell with Vanderbilt," "To hell with Georgia Tech,"
now in Jackson, now in Tuscaloosa, now in Montgomery,
now in Knoxville.

It is an eternal celebration of time defied. The clock on
the field measures no dimension except ritual itself, no
continuity beyond the formal hour of quarters, halves, and
minutes to go. The clock is a liar. Individuals live in other
continuities, but here, in this Southern stadium, in Jackson, Mississippi, the crowd does not. On the Tennessee
side a young woman in an orange suit, with orange
jewelry, orange boots, and an orange ten-gallon hat,
watches the hopeless progress of defeat and screams ob-
scenities at the team, her face contorted with rage. Her
husband, similarly dressed, humiliated now not only by
his costume but by his partner, understands. "Don't be so
hard on those boys," he says to her, loud enough so that
all around can hear. "They're fighting all our battles for
us." It is not a joke. Battles, he knows, can be lost, but
Bruce and Bobby, Charlie and Archie, their achievements
committed to memory, will return eventually, with new
names, to fight the clock another day. The New South is

there, somewhere, in glass and steel and electronics, but this is where youth eternally verifies the past. To defy time is the greatest of heroic acts.

The Negro is time's intruder. From the beginning, the battles were fought by white men while the great Southern black athletes went to Negro colleges which were even more undistinguished academically than the white universities which refused to take them—to the A-and-I's, to Grambling, and Morgan State—and later to the Big Ten, the Big Eight, and the Pacific Coast. Black athletes have begun to predominate in professional football and increasingly in college ball as well, and the Southeastern Conference—Alabama, Auburn, Florida, Georgia, Kentucky, LSU, Ole Miss, Mississippi State, Tennessee, Vanderbilt—has begun to suffer, even if the worshipers at Ole Miss and Alabama don't quite know it yet. A year ago, Bobby Dodd, then the Georgia Tech athletic director, declared patronizingly that "it's just amazing how good the Negro athlete is if given a chance," a remark that must have sounded peculiar—even in the South—at a time when black players had won the National Football League rushing championship six years in succession, the National League baseball batting title seven years of the previous eight, and when virtually every professional basketball star was a Negro.

But Southern football has remained white. The confrontations took place at the schoolhouse door where they were symbolic, not in the stadium or the locker room where they might have gone straight to the heart. The SEC is more than a collection of universities which compete in football and other sports, and winning games, despite assertions to the contrary, may be only one of its considerations; it is the façade, the structure of a ritual where the currents of allegiance run to the bedrock of existence, and where the fantasy of superiority can be maintained not only by regional isolation, but by an athletic schedule that rarely exposes the region's teams to the real behemoths of national football.

In 1965 a few politically astute liberals—people not so much interested in football as in social change—tried to persuade the federal government to bring legal pressure on Deep South universities to recruit and play Negroes: in Alabama, they knew, the most influential man was not George C. Wallace but Paul "Bear" Bryant, the university's football coach. "They didn't understand in Washington that it was important; they were thinking about lofty things like education," one of those liberals said later. "But can you imagine what would have happened if we could have separated Bryant from Wallace, if there had been pictures in the papers of the Bear and some black football star kneeling together in Church?"

Then three years ago—almost, it seemed, by accident— it began to happen, not at Alabama or Ole Miss, but at Kentucky and Tennessee, where the passions of football and race—always running together—were channeled by a sense of the inevitable. Lester McClain, six foot three, one hundred ninety-eight pounds, came from Nashville as Tennessee's first black recruit. There had been abortive efforts to integrate Southern football before; players were recruited but didn't come or didn't stay; some, according to the coaches in the Conference, were academically unqualified, and one quit after playing a few games. McClain, who was signed as a companion to another black player who later withdrew, received the last of Tennessee's quota of football scholarships in 1967. (Football scholarships cover room, board, tuition, and a little free cash;

they are controlled by the coaches, not the university, and it is rare, if not impossible, for a student not on scholarship to play varsity ball.) "The high schools had started to integrate," said Tennessee's head coach, Doug Dickey, "and we figured it was time for us to do something." Since then Dickey has recruited several more; in 1969 three black men were playing varsity ball for Tennessee, Jackie Walker as linebacker, Andy Bennett as a second-string halfback, and McClain as the starting split end. (There are now also a few Negro athletes in other sports—at Tennessee, Auburn, Florida, Kentucky, Georgia Tech, and Mississippi State.) Walker, Bennett, and McClain are all highly skilled athletes, but none is a Jimmy Brown, or an O. J. Simpson. "I think it was easier that way," one of the Tennessee coaches said recently. "The pressure on a superstar would have been that much greater."

Ole Miss leads 21-0, McClain, wearing No. 85, lines up wide to the right, three or four yards beyond the tight end. He cannot hear the snap count of the quarterback, Bobby Scott, over the screaming spectators. When he sees the ball snapped he runs, almost lopes, ten yards downfield, cuts sharply to the inside, and takes the pass from Scott, then turns and gains perhaps another three yards before he is tackled. First down, one of the few Tennessee will get that afternoon. "Hey, Leroy," someone yells from the Ole Miss stands. McClain, who can hear nothing but the crowd, returns to the huddle, "Hey, Leroy," the man screams again. Laughter in the twentieth row. "What you doing givin' that ball to a nigger." Last year, in Knoxville, when Tennessee beat Old Miss 31-0, McClain scored two touchdowns. Some of the Mississippi fans, said one of the Tennessee coaches, were yelling nigger there, too, but McClain didn't hear them either.

McClain never said it was hard; you have to say it for him. It is a long way from the old preacher's place outside Nashville—the thirty acres, the hogs and cows, the seven children spread over two generations—to the University of Tennessee in Knoxville, to Bill Gibbs Hall where the jocks live, to Mississippi Memorial Stadium, where the sun sets behind the banners of the South and the band plays "Dixie." (How did it feel to be playing there, you ask later, and he answers, "I've never seen so many Confederate flags.") For five years the road began at 6:30 A.M. every day, forty miles across the city to the black high school where he started to play football; then, after integration (in his senior year), two hours on a bus every morning, two hours every afternoon; to Antioch High where he learned the style and etiquette of the black player on the white man's field: Don't be the second man on a tackle (he thinks, playing defense for Antioch), some referee might call a penalty (though, in fact, none ever did); don't be obtrusive. "I played ball and people got to know and like me. Then I did the same thing when I got to Tennessee. Maybe the word will get around that black people click just like other people. Maybe the next guys won't have to do this." At first, in the early conversations in the trophy room of the Athletic Building, you think that perhaps he doesn't really know how hard it is, hasn't thought much about what he has to do, or what others are now doing. (Or is he putting you on?) Has he heard about the revolt of the black athletes, the 1968 Olympic boycott, the suspension of black football players at Wyoming and Indiana (and other places) who protested racism in their own schools or among their opponents? Why, he asked at one time, do they always play "Dixie," but he didn't pursue the issue. McClain will have nothing to do with the Black Student Union at Tennessee (there are some 300 black students—of a total of 23,000—on the Knoxville campus), will remain alone rather than mixing too much with anyone, black or white. He doesn't date students at Tennessee; there is a girl at home, and occasionally he spends an evening with girls he meets through "the people who work here," meaning the maids and cooks. Between the lines he tells you that clusters of blacks make him uncomfortable, but he has also learned, somewhere, that the price of integration is not to ask too much of white men either. His roommate, a "fifth-string" quarterback, is white. (Bennett and Walker room together.) "The BSU wanted me to participate in a protest but I didn't understand what they were complaining about. Maybe it's because I live over here with the other athletes, but I didn't have the complaints they had. If I'd wanted black separatism I could have gone to Tennessee A and I." Don't you ever get tired of being unobtrusive, you ask him but he doesn't answer.

> Knoxville (AP)—Tennessee's Lester McClain says being the first Negro to play varsity football in the Southeastern Conference has posed no problems at all.
>
> "I haven't given it any thought," said McClain, who returns to his hometown of Nashville Saturday to play against Vanderbilt. "There have been no problems or incidents of any kind," McClain said. "To the fellows on the team, I feel like I have been just one of the guys from the beginning.
>
> "So far as our opponents are concerned, there have been no problems. Sometimes one of the players will say 'nice block' or 'that was a nice catch.' When we beat Mississippi (in 1968) several of their players sought me out to congratulate me."
>
> McClain was named SEC Lineman of the Week for catching two touchdown passes against Kentucky in Tennessee's 24-7 victory over the Wildcats Saturday. It was

the third time this season McClain had caught two TD passes in a game. He grabbed two against Georgia Tech and two more against UCLA.

On the afternoon before the game, two large buses stop at the side of the empty stadium, and the Tennessee players—for the moment ranked as the sixth-best football team in America—file out, silent in their orange blazers and their too-tight trousers. The cold east wind and the deserted stadium make this a moment of unspeakable loneliness. You have seen lines of young men like this in other places—at induction centers and military schools—and you wonder whether any of them really want to be there. They walk quietly into the dressing room under the concrete stands and reappear on the field a few minutes later, this time in orange sweatsuits and helmets, and begin to run their plays and practice their kicks. (Sometimes, after a good catch or a long kick, they whoop and cheer, but their voices are inadequate to the stadium, and the sound, swept by the wind, is almost meek.) Between plays McClain stands cross-armed, usually alone, warming his hands under his armpits. It is something one usually learns from poverty in cold places.

"What I want to do," McClain had said, "is to make money." He came to college hoping to be an engineer because he had been good in mathematics in high school, "but when I got here, I discovered it was another world, so I switched to accounting." We were sitting on the steps of Gibbs Hall, stopping occasionally to chat with another player. "I had a little trouble in accounting, too, but I'm doing all right now. They'd be talking about some company—the other students knew about it—but living in the country I hadn't even heard of it." He speaks about his childhood, about the brother who runs a successful construction company in Nashville, about a family in which, a decade before, no one could have expected to go to college, let alone to the University of Tennessee. Saturday, for the Georgia Tech game, he will have ten visitors: three brothers, their wives, one of their children, his parents, and his girl who works as a bookkeeper in Nashville. His parents hadn't wanted him to play football, were afraid that he might get hurt, but his brother, now forty-two, encouraged him. When they saw his first press clippings from high school his parents dropped their objections. It was, even then, a possible way out. *Hey, Lester, says a passing player, I saw your picture in the paper again.* "That wasn't me," McClain answers, "that was my brother." What does he talk about with them, you ask, and now he answers a little indefinitely: "Business sometimes, or maybe the high school teams that we follow; or maybe movies or movie stars or music. We talk about girls, but never our own girls, and we never talk about politics. In politics people have different views and it breaks up friendships if you talk about it."

And then, riding in the Olds 442 that his brother gave him, there are dreams and fantasies, but the dreams are tempered by some deep hard sense of reality that seems almost strange on that early fall evening. "I'll play pro football if they pay me for it. Otherwise, I'll stick to accounting; everybody would play pro ball if he had the chance. But what I'd really like to do is be an actor like Jimmy Brown, maybe play in a movie. Not really act, but be in a movie." The world eventually is at the end of some road, in a big city, maybe Atlanta (is that as far as the eye can see?), but not in the rural South, not around here. And then he speaks about the world he is already in, a world in suspension, a world between worlds: "I went back to a game at a black high school in Memphis and felt like a stranger. If I went to an all-white affair I'd feel like a stranger, too. I feel at home in a place that's integrated."

We stopped at Shoney's Restaurant for ice cream, the black athlete from Nashville, the Jewish writer from New York, talking now about how people grow up, how kids learn, about life in the streets and in the country, and about the subtle things one has to learn, each of you knowing that in a situation like this some things must be left unsaid. McClain tells of the Cotton Bowl game in Dallas the previous New Year's Day: there had been some hope that if Tennessee was up and Texas down it might be a close game, but it turned out to be the other way around, and Texas won easily. During the week in Dallas, McClain said, "Some of the guys went clubbing. I didn't like Dallas —everybody walking around in ten-gallon hats and cowboy boots. I don't want to wear a ten-gallon hat and I didn't go clubbing. Some of the guys asked me to go along; I thought it was nice of them to ask me." (What, you wonder, was left unsaid?) "There wasn't anything to do in Dallas; I didn't know where to go, didn't know any places, so I went home the day after the game." Then what's the point of it all, what's the use, you ask, and he says it does make a difference. "I know one guy—from Selma; his daddy won't have anything to do with black people. He told how he's discovered that black people click just like other people. He asked me to his wedding."

The waitress brings our check—McClain has to get back to his dormitory for the 11 P.M. curfew. "It's been real nice serving you," says the waitress, like a recorded announcement.

Tennessee has just beaten Georgia Tech 26-8. In the team meeting room outside the showers, the orange carpet is littered with pieces of discarded tape and cans of Gator-

ade. Three or four young boys—all of them white—stop McClain on his way out, ask for his autograph, and wait quietly while he signs on programs and scraps of paper. He walks on toward the door leading into the stadium, meeting Walker and Bennett near the exit, and the three emerge together. Outside there are more autographs for waiting boys, handshakes from the parents of some of the other players, and an embrace from Marcia, the girl from Nashville. Bennett and Walker go on together; McClain and Marcia walk alone across the field, up the steps on the other side, and finally into the street. On the way they are stopped several more times—handshakes, congratulations, introductions—and when they arrive at the reception outside Gibbs Hall (held after each home game), they are absorbed into the chatter of the crowd, into the orange blazers and the tailored autumn dresses. It is like a fraternity party on a homecoming weekend, now familiar and jocular, now formal and awkward. At the edge of the crowd Andrew McClain, the older brother, tells Lester of the family plans to drive to Birmingham for the Alabama game, and then, when Lester and Marcia stop to talk to the fiancée of one of the other players, Andrew speaks about his own youth during the depression. "Lester," he said, "will have it a little better." Resting against the fender of a parked car, McClain's seventy-year-old father, his wrinkled hands folded across his middle, looks absently at the orange pompom that Marcia brought back from the game.

If football is the major ritual of the South—its religion, its dream, its secret life—it is also a world unto itself, a million-dollar enterprise directed by professionals, played by "amateurs" (for pride, for money, for an education), and surrounded by hordes of managers, publicists, soothsayers, and assorted hangers-on, paid and unpaid, who live in the reflected glory of Saturday afternoon. One does not have to remain among them long to understand how bruised hips, pulled groin muscles, and twisted knees can become Major Events, how and why athletes—black and white—become chattel, or why, for that very reason, the one-dimensional assessment of players takes on that fundamental honesty which is interested, above all, in winners. All these things make it easier to integrate Negro athletes than Negro students: if every man is property, if self-effacement, good conduct and discipline (not to mention strength and speed) are the highest virtues, then one can treat Negroes and athletes in precisely the same way. They're all boys. But for that reason, also, the Negro athlete may turn out to be the Trojan horse in the locker room. If he decides to rebel in the name of black freedom, how long will it take the white players to decide that they're niggers, too, and that curfews, dress codes, and special dormitories are for children, for boys, not for men?

It is all there, the breaking-in, and, somewhere in the distance, the breaking-up, and between them, the rumors, hypotheses, and innuendos of change. "I don't understand what's the matter with mankind," says a sportswriter from Nashville. "They're all crazy, letting those good colored players go North. The best thing that's happened to this place is getting Lester McClain. You know what Bear Bryant told me? He told me Southeastern Conference football would never be great again until they removed the restrictions."

What restrictions?

"I don't know that they got any rules; it's just that there might be trouble, but people would accept it, just like they accepted it here. They keep saying that the colored players can't make it academically, but that's just an excuse. They're all taking players who aren't geniuses."

"Why don't they take them in under the poverty program?" says a visiting football scout from the Dallas Cow-
boys. "If they can't qualify under SEC rules [The
Conference imposes minimum standards for athletes]
they'd have a year for remedial work. Then, if they don't
flunk out, you could give 'em football scholarships."

"Lester's just perfect," says another sportswriter. "He
must have been raised well. His father's a preacher down
in Nashville."

What about the revolt of the black athletes elsewhere?

"Oh, you can tell," says the scout. "You can spot the
troublemakers."

The hypotheses abound and the rumors flow, and the
variables become almost too numerous to manage: coaches
are professionals who want to win, and will play anyone
who can help them do it; the people of Mississippi and
Alabama, perhaps even the people of Tennessee, would
never support teams dominated by black players; it is
better not to get stars who are black since they would be
too threatening to the faithful; it is imperative to get stars
if you are going to recruit black players at all, so there
is no doubt that their scholarships and their presence on
the team are justified. And as the recognition of the potential value of black athletes increases, so do the defenses.
"Sure, those black boys can run," said someone from Ole
Miss, "because they're built differently, their legs are different. It's their bones. Houston had a fellow—I can't remember his name—he could run, but he was yellow." The
Conference rules, you are told by the reasonable people,
have made it difficult for black athletes to qualify academically, yet there is no evidence that SEC regulations
are more stringent than those in any other conference.
Somehow Dickey has managed to get Negro players while

Bryant at Alabama and Johnny Vaught at Ole Miss have not. (In the fall of 1969 Mississippi State played two outstanding black athletes in its freshman football game against Ole Miss; Mississippi State won 51-0 and that may create more pressure than all the civil rights cases in the world.) "We're seeking athletes regardless of color," said Vaught. "We signed a couple [meaning they had signed letters of intent—minicontracts], but one didn't qualify academically and the other decided to go elsewhere. We would have liked the boy from Vicksburg [now the starting quarterback at Michigan State]. He's an exceptionally fine boy." Vaught claims that he has sought athletes at all-black high schools in the state ("They're all supposed to be integrated now," he said), but there is considerable doubt about the diligence of his pursuit. Ole Miss fans, said Vaught, would support the team even if there were black players—after all, he added, there are many Negro students on campus—but others in Oxford aren't so sure. "They'd accept it," said someone on the Ole Miss staff, "but they sure as hell wouldn't like it." Whatever the hypotheses (Could any black man, indeed, play for a team calling itself the Rebels; could any crowd waving Confederate flags cheer his touchdown?), the fact is simply that there are no black players. In Jackson a gentleman representing the White Citizen's Council was asked if the council had a policy about black and white athletes playing on the same team. "No," he said, "we don't have a policy on that. But I'll make one up. We're against it."

On Thursday they begin to assemble: the advance men, the early travelers, the big-bellied men with their carbuncular class rings, the bourbon-pickled loud-voiced women, debouching from Cadillacs and chartered planes, how-ya-doin' through the lobbies of motels, starting the *party, greeting the arrivals—To hell with ole Miss, To hell with Tennessee. "City Greets Vols for Nippy Reb Tiff." Each week they march through the South, armies of the faithful, forsaking their vacations for six or ten three-day football weekends, carrying their cushions, their bottles, their loneliness, possessed by what they can no longer possess, filling the void with noise. "Wasn't that a helluva game . . . we kicked to 'em but it hardly went past the line of scrimmage . . . Missed you in Memphis . . . The lot's right at the bottom of the hill, you turn right . . . You know Mrs. Davis, and this is her sister . . . "To Hell With Tennessee." Sometimes they charter trains: $100, Knoxville to Birmingham, for sleepers, club car, two breakfasts and Saturday dinner, sometimes they fly or drive. "In Birmingham or Jackson you can feel the electricity, the excitement," someone had said. "They're really proud of those teams: maybe it's because they haven't had much else to be proud of." If this is what it's like to be an adult, who would ever want to grow up? To Hell With Ole Miss. Mississippi goddam. By the time they arrive at the game, they have given voice to the secret meaning, have, as it were, invented words for what words can't express. (It happens to be, through ironic coincidence, Youth Appreciation Week.) The big grudge, the longings and passions denied, cannot be played out, for when youth ends, so does life, and so little grudges, which can be adjudicated here and now, must replace them. Before the season began, a sportswriter has observed that Ole Miss seemed to have the horses for another good year, and Steve Kiner, Tennessee's All American linebacker, countered that some people can't tell horses from mules. It was the sort of remark that nice boys aren't supposed to make, an insult, if you will, to the race, and it helped give this game its higher cause. Archie Manning, Mississippi's sanctified* *quarterback, moreover, had been reduced, on buttons worn by Tennessee rooters, to "Archie Who?"*

Going into the game, Tennessee is undefeated, with a record of 7-0; Ole Miss has lost three, one of them to the University of Houston, whose team is integrated. When the announcer reads the starting lineups at Mississippi Memorial Stadium, he lists only ten starters for the Tennessee offense. McClain's name is omitted. At the same moment, according to the papers, Richard M. Nixon is preparing to watch Ohio State–Purdue on television, and the 500,000 people who came to Washington to protest the Vietnam war are gathering for their final rally. "Cops Use Tear Gas on D. C. Marchers." In Mississippi Memorial Stadium, a local minister reads the invocation: "God be with our fighting men in Vietnam who are fighting to keep our country free. In Jesus' name, Amen." The Ole Miss band plays the Star Spangled Banner, and 47,000 people begin to scream, waiting for the battle.

In the background hangs the specter of change and revolt, not merely among black athletes, but among all young men and women. References to riots and demonstrations creep incessantly into the discussions of collegiate sports, and you are reminded, without ever having asked, that the orderly, disciplined life of the athlete is far more conducive to "getting an education" than the turmoil of a disrupted campus. "How can you study," someone said, "if the university is closed down or the students are sitting in? The rooms in Gibbs Hall are kept clean; there are no drugs. These boys here have a chance to learn." On the Tennessee campus itself, several hundred students chartered buses to attend the second Vietnam Moratorium; the use of marijuana is extensive and the number of freaks—people given to long hair, beads, and joss sticks—grows every year. On the evening after the Georgia Tech game they held an outdoor "Freak Concert" —bands, folk singers, guitars—attended by five or six hundred people who were not above shouting "Kill the pig" when the campus police car came around. And while Doug Dickey quietly integrated his football team, the undergraduates themselves elected Jimmie Baxter, a black Air Force veteran, as president of the Student Government. (At the University of Alabama, Diane Kirksy, a Negro, was one of the three finalists for 1969 homecoming queen—the ultimate winner was a Japanese American named Sue Shimoda—and at LSU the Student Government Association asked the University athletic director to begin active recruitment of black athletes).

What you learn from people like Baxter (and from the freaks) is that slowly the base of student support, even at Tennessee, is beginning to erode beneath the old forms and institutions, and that new rituals—the ceremonial passing of the joint, for example—have started to replace them. In the months before Baxter's election there had been several protests—on women's hours, an open speaker policy, and Black Studies—which helped focus student sentiment. "I ran against the usual fraternity candidates," said Baxter (wearing an Afro, beard, shades, and a blue denim jacket). "I was the only one who raised the issue of student power, and I got elected. This place is changing." As you talk with people like him you reestablish contact with the newer student world, people who speak about the Vietnam war, and about reform. "The students aren't half as turned on about football as they were a few years ago. Football is still supported—by the alumni, the administration, the trustees, by the whole state. The students know it's there, and most of them go to the games, but they're not as wild about it as they used to be. These people come into the

Student Center on Saturday before the games in their orange suits and coats, with their Tennessee neckties, and they stare at the freaks with their long hair. But they haven't any idea how silly *they* look. They'll support a team with a few black players ("Everyone's for Lester," said someone else, "because he's *our* nigger"), but if we got too many they'd begin to wonder if it was really their team. And we're never likely to have a black quarterback. That's not the role they imagine for Negroes."

And every day, the national black revolt comes closer. What Harry Edwards, then a teacher at San Jose State College, began in organizing the 1968 Olympic protest (first against participation by South Africa, then against U.S. racism) has spread to major institutions in nearly every part of the country: black athletes demanding more black coaches and teachers, refusing to participate in competition against what they regard as racist opponents, insisting on better academic conditions—among them Black Studies programs—and better treatment on the campus.

> Gradually [wrote Edwards in his book *The Revolt of the Black Athlete*] most black college athletes begin to realize that their white employers, their teammates, even their fellow students, in spite of the cheers and adulations they shower upon them, regard them as something akin to super animals, but animals nevertheless . . . A black athlete on a white campus cannot afford to make mistakes or perform occasionally at a mediocre level. If he does, he does not play.
>
> If he fails academically, he is ridiculed; but if he quits he is despised. For he has not taken advantage of "the chance that his parents didn't have." He has failed those who had faith in him . . . A black athlete himself may feel guilty even about the thought of quitting. But what he doesn't realize is that he can never prove himself in the eyes of white racists—not at any rate, as a man or even a

human being. From their perspective he is, and always will be, a nigger. From their perspective the only difference between the black man shining shoes in the ghetto and the champion black sprinter is that the shoeshine man is a nigger, while the sprinter is a fast nigger.

The black athlete on the white-dominated college campus . . . is typically exploited, abused, dehumanized, and cast aside in much the same manner as a worn basketball.

The voices in the athletic offices intone the words "no trouble" like an incantation against evil spirits. Counting track runners, Tennessee now has eleven black athletes on scholarship: track integrated before football. "You have to take into consideration what kind of guys these Negroes are. They're not marching or protesting. (You know some guys have an inferiority complex about being colored.) These guys fit right in. The fans have kind of adopted them." The coaches cannot bring themselves to believe that there will be trouble here, or at least not to discuss it. They treat their players equitably, and they believe in the validity of the order they maintain. "The revolt of the black athletes will be a passing thing," Dickey said. "They're following undisciplined leadership. The only place on the campus where there's still discipline is in athletics and fraternities. ROTC is almost gone in most places. It's sad that Negroes as a race lack stable leadership. But there's been no problem here. Sure, there have been some confrontations, between black and white, and between white and white, but football players, you have to remember, are combative types, and some of them can't always keep it on the field."

By the time the Tennessee offense gets the ball the first time, Ole Miss has already scored and the crowd is yelling for more. High in the Ole Miss stands someone has hung a hand-lettered banner: "No Fruit Sucks Like a Big Orange." McClain lines up wide to the right; Scott gives the ball to Curt Watson, the fullback, who cracks into the line for perhaps two yards. McClain, blocking downfield, hits the defensive halfback, Wyck Neely, a junior from Magee, Mississippi, drives him backward, and knocks him down, but Watson has already been stopped. McClain helps Neely up, and trots back to the huddle. Two plays later, on third and long yardage, McClain runs a pass pattern, ten yards downfield and clear, but Scott, looking for one of his other receivers, doesn't see him, and fails to make the completion. On the way back upfield, one of the Ole Miss defensive backs gives McClain a friendly pat on the rump. On fourth down, a bad punt gives Ole Miss the ball on the Tennessee 38, and a few plays later the Rebels score again.

The clock moves. During the Tennessee–Georgia Tech game, a sportswriter from Memphis was quick to point out to the visiting Yankee journalist that the band playing "Dixie" was not Tennessee's but Georgia Tech's. Does he know why there are no Negro cheerleaders, has he heard the story about the white girl who told a Negro applicant not to come back unless she brought her own black man so that no white boy would have to toss a black girl in the air? Sitting in a small campus office, Ralph Boston, a 1968 Olympic medal winner in the long jump, now an assistant dean of students (and one of the few black men on the Tennessee staff), speaks about change. "It's coming here, too. You have to make some adjustments. If you're going to take black athletes or black students you can't just go on in the old way, expecting black kids to stand up when they play "Dixie" or to accept the Confederate flag. It's silly to say that a kid can't play with a beard or a mustache, whether he's black or white. Joe Namath wins games with a mustache. I think some of these kids are angry, but they can't say much because they have to make it themselves first. There's a story about O. J. [Simpson]; he was supposed to have told the kids in Watts, 'Give me three or four years to make it, to make a real name as a football player, and I'll be back to help you.' But of course three or four years is a long time."

McClain says very little. They are all cordial, the athletes, the coaches, the flacks, but life around an athletic dormitory doesn't permit much privacy. One must learn, in this helpful, hospitable despotism, to keep one's mouth shut. "I don't think the papers are really telling very much about what's going on," he said one day at lunch. "One of the white guys on the team was saying that there must be something to the protest at Wyoming; they just wouldn't be doing all this without a cause." For people like McClain, football is the road to a better life, a means to an end. Some of the other black athletes, he said, have been doing some thinking, "but it wouldn't help 'em to say anything." For the coming summer, McClain himself already has several job offers from accounting firms "because they can't find enough black accountants." He is, as he hoped, on the way to "another class of life."

"What are you angry about?" you ask him for perhaps the third time, but there is still no answer. And then, for a moment, McClain speaks about Lew Alcindor, the great black basketball star who, after graduation, wrote about the racism he encountered while playing for UCLA. "You know," said McClain finally, "some day I'd like to tell my story the way Alcindor did."

*A minute before the half, with the score 24-0, Scott
attempts a long pass to McClain who is a step or two
behind the man who is covering him, but the ball is under-
thrown and the pass intercepted. "Hey, Nigger," shouts a
young man from an end-zone seat, "you be goin' to Jackson
State with the other niggers." By now it is clear that the
defeat is turning into a rout, and the crowd is beginning
to celebrate. Everything is coming together again, the flag,
the race, the time. The band marches, the eunuch steps
and foppish costumes prancing in unmanly counterpoint
to the gladiators in the main event. "You're always hoping
for the big play, hoping you can do something," McClain
said later, but in the second half nothing changes. Kiner,
still suffering from an injury, plays poorly, Walker is arm
tackling, letting ball carriers run past him, and Archie
Manning, never better, moves his team for two more
touchdowns. The crowd, responding to the Archie buttons, begins to chant "Kiner Who? Kiner Who? Kiner
Who?" (later some of them will send him vicious little
postcards), while in the Ole Miss cheering section the students yell rhythmically, "No School on Monday, No School
on Monday." In Washington, at this moment, other kids
are singing the songs of peace and listening to the last
moratorium speakers plead for withdrawal, and you remember how, a few weeks before, McClain, appearing at
a pre-game pep rally had made V with his fingers, explain-
ing that "usually this means peace, but on a Friday night,
it stands for victory," remember how the white children
of the fraternities and sororities responded with their
ritual cheers in the autumn night." In the last moments of
the game Ole Miss intercepts a desperate pass by a second-
string Tennessee quarterback, and as the Mississippi sub-
stitutes go in to kill the clock, the defensive players,*

flushed, bouncing with triumph, come off the field and flash the V to their cheering fans. As the crowd disperses, Ross Barnett, former governor of Mississippi, pale and ghostlike, wanders around the end zone, greeting the scattered people who recognize him, and shouts "Archie for governor."

[1969]

WHITE MAN
IN HARLEM

Every white man is a stranger in Harlem. But any one of us who remains there too long or goes too often also becomes a stranger to his own place and perhaps to himself, a man unhinged, wondering now if Harlem is real or just the creature of a literary imagination, wondering again if anything else is real or if the rest of the world is the dream and its inhabitants the dreamers.

For more than a year I have been making the crossing: downtown-uptown, uptown-downtown, and from the cool commuter trains of the New York Central to the intensity of 125th Street, traversing a psychic barrier that has no parallel in ordinary transformations of awareness. No matter how often it is done, each crossing makes one a racial alien whose skin betrays his mind. After two days in the ghetto I regard the commuters on the White Plains local as a race apart, a distant culture, a crowd I subtly detest. And each return to Harlem is a reminder of another estrangement, the white man in the black town, fearful and uncertain, trying to determine how—and if—any of his brothers and predecessors managed, under similar circumstances, to remain untouched.

To believe that Harlem really exists is to learn the horror of being white in contemporary America. I am not speaking here of guilt, or of the uncertainties produced by the varied responses of the black men and women one encounters: How much is guile and con, how much rage, how much envy or affection? How much has sheer disdain for a white man also become invisible? Talk about three hundred years of slavery and oppression doesn't stir, in me, any feeling of racial culpability. I want to be honored with a personal indictment, and perhaps have earned it, but if an angry man attacks me on some black street, it will be the absurd murder of someone who is being tried but does not yet feel convicted.

I came trying to understand the community and what it teaches its children and adults, and have learned a great deal, but I still don't understand and feel now that I probably never shall. Yet I have come to terms with Harlem, and in doing so I discover that the place has become part of the furniture of my consciousness, become part of me. I have the rage without the suffering that would establish my right to have it. I assume that this is not unique; there must be hundreds of whites who have become psychic or racial nomads in this country; you meet them on the periphery of community action programs and

in tutoring centers, survivors of a civil rights mov
working diligently to demonstrate loyalty to a cause
has a growing desire to declare them superfluous.

The horror derives from the fact that insofar as race
defines any set of social problems in America, the action,
vitality, and initiative—and hence the freedom—are black.
What this means, I think, is that Black Power has not only
established itself as an idea, but that it has already begun
to turn psychic tables on the whites. Liberal intellectuals
have always had a tenuous kinship with my commuters,
rarely identified with television heroes, and have certainly ceased to regard the history of Western civilization
as an uninterrupted chronicle of ascending triumphs. In
some respects, surely, they are as alien to white culture as
the black kids who have so little common ground with the
official world. Yet I think that what scares the liberals
most is the real possibility that black power has begun to
steal their virulence and courage. (That is, of course, also
what scares them about student revolts.) They are supposed to be the initiators, the critics, the cranks. The
blacks are forcing them into that—for them—most revolting of positions: defense of the Establishment.

Harlem is the source. Certainly it is a black ghetto like
many others, and surely it is neither the largest nor the
worst (whatever that means) among them. Detroit and
Watts have demonstrated that sociological statistics and
community programs devised by political officials are
sorry indicators of good and bad in ghetto conditions.
(Those conditions are, in many cases, defined by the attitudes and practices of the world outside. I doubt if Harlem
would be regarded as a slum in Calcutta.) Nonetheless,
Harlem is *it*. Harlem is the capital, the spiritual home of
black men, even if they never left the plantation. "Harlem," wrote Harold Cruse in *The Crisis of the Negro Intel-*

lectual, "is the black world's key community for historical, political, economic, cultural and/or ethnic reasons. The trouble is that Harlem has never been adequately analyzed in such terms. The demand often heard—'Break up the Harlem ghetto!' (as a hated symbol of segregation)— represents nothing but the romantic and empty wail of politically insolvent integrationists, who fear ghetto riots only more than they fear the responsibilities of political and economic power that lie in the Harlem potential . . ." Harlem had (and to some extent still has) a culture that now flows into the mainstream. The jazz has gone downtown, the old Savoy has long disappeared, replaced by a supermarket; Langston Hughes is dead; Ralph Ellison lives on the West Side and belongs to the Century Club; James Baldwin, not long ago described to be "as angry as a man can get," has a million-dollar book contract. And if you want to see Nina or Ella or Harry Belafonte, your chances are better at the Persian Room than at the Apollo on 125th Street. Still, Harlem is the source. It has provided America with its social vocabulary, its musical idiom, with a worldly self-awareness beyond the ebullient clichés of history. In its fusion of Southern and urban modes, in its distillation of suffering, and the consciousness of suffering, in its ducts to New York's literary and intellectual sensibilities, it has become the forge of cultural and political styles and attitudes that shape Negro—and white—life everywhere in America. Harlem has begun to restore humility to affluence, humanity to arrogance. It threatens to take American life out of its polyethylene sterility, to introduce to it the tragic, the absurd, the imponderable. For the first time we are beginning to suspect that suffering is not a problem but a condition.

Harlem has no beginning or end. It has been said that Harlem starts in Alabama and Trinidad, and that it extends to the suburbs of Los Angeles and the jungles of Vietnam. Part of what makes it peculiar to New Yorkers is not Negro but Southern; part of what makes it confusing is not black but American. There are Mississippi whites who have felt more at home on Lenox Avenue than native New York liberals who live just a few blocks away. Columbia University, separated from the black community by a narrow park, topographical elevation, and some real estate maneuvers is more distant than Yoknapatawpha County. Harlem's religion, its penchant for high life, and its violence germinated in the black soil of the South, not on the pavements of the city.

In many respects it is not a place at all, certainly not a community, despite the rhetoric of those militants who like to talk of what "the community wants." More than anything it is a state of mind, and we have all become its carriers. The American panic about crime in the streets, about urban riots, indicates that one no longer has to go there to be there. Harlem's uncertainty about itself—about whether it wants to be in or out, whether it will be violent or docile, whether there is value in being middle-class—is also my uncertainty. Although I don't know what I would like it to be, it has become too much part of me to leave it alone. One can penetrate through layers of romance about black culture and statistics of deprivation and arrive at a blank wall whose only escape is bias. Because Harlem is America, part of its mounting anger can be attributed to *its* inability to escape, and to the fact that much of its nationalistic liturgy won't serve as anything but a temporary incantation against white devils. We are, in short, prisoners together, each defining himself by the other, neither of us complete by himself.

The problem of Harlem is, immediately, the problem of cacophony, of filtering sound from noise, of distinguishing the Aesopian from the sociological, of separating passion from propaganda. Every conversation, every street scene, every sidewalk pitchman throws up a cosmos, angry, sycophantic, conspiratorial, insulting, amusing, style against style, rhythm against rhythm. Muslims in brocaded caps, men in turquoise pants and orange shirts, women in rhinestone-studded slacks, children dodging traffic to fly kites, playing basketball with peach baskets hung on the fire escapes, souped-up checker games in the playgrounds, leaflets, *Muhammad Speaks*, CORE, Urban League, numbers, the Supremes and James Brown and Aretha Franklin from the record-store loudspeakers, Brother Lewis Michaux in the back of his African nationalist bookstore telling how "the politicians pacify, the preachers sanctify, and the white man crucifies."

The preachers and the spiritualists grow rank—Madam Martha and Sister Marie, Bishops of the World, prophets, healers, pitchmen—rhetoricians of the gospels, sellers of indulgences, tough talking Mau Maus, foghorned mamas, pushers and pushed, a jungle of organizations and committees, sects and movements. In the Gothic novel one would make his way through these peripheries to some dark heart, an inner secret, but here there is no secret, and that, in itself, is Harlem's most intimate possession.

Harlem is a collection: layers, networks, labyrinths—the dark alley of the American spirit—and to an outsider it is just as confounding as the Casbah or the Sicilian village. In part it suffers from sociological pollution—a territory covered by the muddy tracks of welfare investigators, professors, journalists counting heads, making notes, asking questions, seeking symptoms and cures of a disease that draws its poison from other places and other roots. The basic statistics are simple, and we can all recite them: 300,000 souls, give or take a few thousand who bob below the vision of the census, a fourth of them without jobs, broken families, poor education, poor housing, poor health. But they obfuscate more than they clarify because they flatten complexity and variety into a useless average. Despite the growing anger, despite the put-ons, one can still feel accepted, can be received into homes and hear stories of ambitions and struggles, can attend meetings and services, yet never get more than a fragmentary map of the community, a view through a hole in the ice. The block, not the neighborhood, defines for most people the limits of place and belonging. The woman who has lived for a decade on 119th Street will never move, if she has a choice, because, as she tells you, "Here I feel safe." She will defend that block; any change imposed by the outside is likely to be for the worse. When urban renewal comes, it not only puts human beings out of familiar surroundings, it also destroys sources of strength and familiarity, old associations, and established patterns of life. The junkies and winos move to the next block, and new protective habits must be developed. Every child in Harlem masters the streets and alleys of his neighborhood, knows every store and often every resident. "When I was a kid," said a Harlem teacher, "I could walk around my neighborhood blindfolded." Within such settings there develops a local leadership, block leadership, that never registers on the radar screens of the outside world. These are the people who take care of the kids next door, raise money for the funeral or to ship the body down South, and who staff the networks of neighborhood councils, parents organizations, and protest committees that lace every precinct. There are no questions that one can ask of them. What they can communicate we already know. What we should learn they cannot tell us. Where they are lame we are blind. For them black power is beside the point. There is, after all, nothing else; there never has been. Certainly they have not survived on white justice, or even on white charity.

It is a place of environs and styles, in fashion, in speech, in architecture, but one of its central facts, it seems to me, is style itself, a thing done with grace and flourish—Willie Mays catching a fly ball, an elegant riff on the trumpet, an outfit that stops the show. It is the curious impression that, for its size and poverty, Harlem seems to be full of establishments that rent tuxedos. On Upper Fifth Avenue it is a woman in a green pants suit, green shoes, and black derby hat walking a poodle, and two blocks away in the playground at 142nd and Lenox it is the beat and speed of a checker game, one of several surrounded by spectators, where the *click, click, click* of the jumping pieces play a counterpoint to the separate monologues of the players. "Now what you want me to do?" *Click, click.* "Now what you want me to do?" *Click, click.* "I'll take care of that one later." *Click, click, click.* A double jump, *click, click,* answered by a triple jump, *click, click, click* and "Crown me!"

The style of Harlem is in the pride young boys develop in their toughness, in their ability to withstand pain without complaint, in the joy and laughter of children, in the mastery of the hustler, and in the uninhibited phrase-making of a street orator. "Around here," said Wilbert Kirby of CORE, "they got guys that can sell anything, and if they got nothin' to sell, they'll try to sell you nothin'. They have this con; they learned it from the masters. I remember a guy who was trying to sell a man a miff—a miff, now what the hell is that? Why there ain't no such thing. Why the hell doesn't General Motors hire these con men to sell cars? They've got the best experience in the world."

Style, I suspect, is one of the ultimate defenses against

the all too insistent brutality of discrimination and disregard. Sharp clothes, if they serve no other purpose, make poverty bearable, may symbolize a small beachhead on the shores of affluence. For all of us, the automobile talks back to boredom and emptiness, promises escape, even if it never delivers. More important, however, Harlem is a repository of style and taste, not only in music and dance but in clothes and canapés and floral arrangements. As a slave and servant, the American Negro learned the style of the aristocrat long before he learned to be middle-class; he thus became, and to some extent still remains, the carrier of elegance and refinement in America. To claim this too stridently is to lay oneself open to accusations of romance from Marxist judges of social welfare. Yet surely we still live in a time when black maids and handymen, with all their aches and superstitions, often rescue suburban housewives by turning their domestic kitsch to culture.

If there is any continuity here—the sort of continuity that can be discerned by white eyes—it is in the interface between Soul and civilization. Each, it seems to me, is at war with itself, but each, more significantly, is at war with the other. Soul, finally, is anti-civilization, uncompromising passion, human instinct and experience before they have been subjugated and disciplined. Civilization is repressive, foreign, a white man's trick. Each of us, as Freud made clear, struggles with those issues, but Harlem, and the black revolt everywhere else, has given them new life and has extended their dimensions from the psychological to the political. Soul is not merely music or style or a form of black brotherhood; it is human reality uncontaminated by social demand and sociological strategy. Soul is simultaneously the dream of life before the fall—supremely American, the vision of the new man in a virgin land, free of the corruptions of the old world—*and* a statement of depths of experience and feeling that only fellow sufferers can understand. Either way, it stands apart from civilized convention, from civilization itself, questioning, challenging, demanding.

The struggle is not merely internal, though I suspect that anyone carrying a Molotov cocktail after the murder of Martin Luther King must have experienced it; it is also a contest between groups, styles of life, and varieties of commitment. "Everybody around here," said a young member of CORE, "is looking. The gutter types want to be grassroots types, the grassroots types want to be middle-class, and the middle-class wants to be white." There is continuity between the bottom and the mainstream, but there is also resistance—Africanism, Black Awareness, schools of Swahili and a whole demonology cataloguing the deviltry of the white man. Speak to any three groups, and you get three different versions of the universe, each of them certified to be The Real Black View. Nonetheless, they share what most of us have only achieved in the loftier reaches of rhetoric—an attempt to come to terms with an urban life for which America has yet to conceive a point of view.

If all this suggests that I regard Harlem as an exotic place, or that I ignore its shabbiness, its agonies, or its powerful middle-class ambitions, let me set the matter straight. Harlem is too American to be exempt from any of that; its anger does not derive from its other-worldliness: we are not dealing with Indian mystics or medieval saints, but with American dreamers denied their frontier. The growing rage only makes sense in the context of hypocritical invitations and frustrated ambition. In cutting through to the bedrock of racism, it was inevitable, as Eldridge Cleaver has said, that leadership would eventually shift from the house niggers to the field niggers, from those whose position derived from a relationship with the master to those who had neither influence nor access to the established seats of power. What this means is that, in the long run, the rhetoric will become more reliable, less manipulative, and at the same time, harder to take. The test for the militants—the field niggers—will be in their ability to channel and control the violence of the community. That violence is not new, but as Fanon and Malcolm X have pointed out, it was always directed against other victims of the oppressor's brutality: blacks killing blacks, turning their rage against each other, sparing the exploiter, and giving him new ground to assert his superiority. The leadership of nonviolence was buried with Martin Luther King. There is no one else left, except the young militants. For them, the problem is whether they can control their own neighborhoods or whether we will all be dealing with a mob.

Norman Mailer has written that the militant Negro "does not want equality any longer, he wants superiority, and wants it because he feels he is in fact superior. And there is some justice on his side for believing it. Sufficiently fortunate to be alienated from the benefits of American civilization, the Negro seems to have been better able to keep his health. It would take a liberal with a psychotic sense of moderation to claim that whites and Negroes have equally healthy bodies; the Negroes know they have become on the average physically superior, and this *against all the logic of America's medical civilization*—the Negroes get less good food ostensibly, no vitamins, a paucity of antibiotics, less medical care, less fresh air, less light and sanitation in living quarters. Let us quit the list—it is parallel to another list one could make of educational opportunities vs. actual culture (which is to say—real awareness of one's milieu). The Negro's relatively low rate of literacy seems to be in inverse relation to his philosophical capacity to have a comprehensive vision of his life, a large remark whose only support is existential—let us brood, brothers, on the superior cool of the Negro in public places. For the cool comes from a comprehensive vision, a relaxation before the dangers of life, a readiness to meet death, philosophy or amusement at any turn."

Unless Mailer is referring to the smallest of minorities, he is not describing the people I have met and interviewed: housewives and block leaders trying to keep the junkies off the street and the cops honest; bankers promoting economic development; teachers talking about jobs and education and housing; community organizers checking food prices in supermarkets and installment interest rates on junk furniture. Harlem is not merely a reproach to the mainstream, a product of its atrocities, but also an affirmation. The private middle-class housing developments of Lenox Terrace and Riverbend, the elegance of the Stanford White houses on Strivers Row, the brownstones on Sugar Hill near City College make it abundantly clear that one part of militancy is a loud rap on the door to affluence. There are too many people who want in, who have college ambitions for their children, and who have become gymnasts on the exercise bars of the middle class to make Harlem exotic or to make Mailer's assertion acceptable.

What makes Mailer's statement notable is not what it says about black men but about whites, about the experience of being a white man in Harlem. We are no longer living in white America but in a country infiltrated by moral guerrillas demanding acceptance of our common Negritude. I know of no way that an ordinary white man can come to understand Harlem unless he understands the repressed and conflicting passions that he shares with its inhabitants. This is more than saying the Negro problem is a white problem, or that Harlem's resolution depends on Scarsdale. It is, rather, to confront those parts of our own lives that are unlivable, to see our own empty spaces. The problem is not the suburban community, but the suburban heart.

As a political philosophy, Black Power is, finally, a simple idea that smacks of nothing so much as Calhoun's doctrine of the concurrent majority. Where Calhoun wanted political parity for a minority of ante-bellum slave states, the black militant wants it for the Negro ghetto. But Black Power contains a moral component that makes it more than a political strategy. One of the most obvious and striking things about Harlem is the visible decay of the rural culture—religion, school, even family—that gave Negro life its tenuous stability in the South. What survives is the Jeffersonian reproach to urban brutality, and what grows from it is a search for an urban ethic beyond politics and welfare. The black militant scolds the white Establishment in the tone and cadences of the black mammy, but what he demands is the kind of compensation that has value only if it hurts. The solution for Harlem is not the diversion of surplus wealth or an annual Saturday-afternoon paint job, but shared suffering. In some way we must all learn to die for our sins. And to live and laugh again, too.

[1968]

ERIE: LIFE ON A DYING LAKE

North Central flight 940. We take off to the west from the Detroit Metro Airport, turn left in a large loop around the city, and emerge over the crotch of the Detroit River where the patterned effluent spills into the waiting blue water of Lake Erie. *Two weeks before the final countdown for Apollo XI, the supreme $24 billion apotheosis of American technology; the greatest thing, Richard Nixon will say, since the Creation.* The brown waters hug the western shore, and beyond, through the thin haze from the Michigan stacks, the ore carriers cut white wakes to feed the factories. We cross the rectilinear fields of Pelee Island and pass Pelee Point on the Ontario shore to the north. Less than 150 miles to the south is Wapakoneta, Ohio, where the first man to set foot on the moon was born.

> Man is destroying Lake Erie. [Says the report from the Federal Water Pollution Control Administration.] Although the accelerating destruction process has been inadvertent, it is as positive as if he had put all his energies into devising and implementing the means. After two generations the process has gained a momentum which now requires a monumental effort to retard. The effort must not only be basin-wide and highly coordinated; it must be immediate. Every moment lost in allowing the destruction to continue will require a longer, more difficult, and more expensive corrective action.

Prosaic language from Washington: eutrophication, secondary treatment, nutrient removal, algal blooms, biological oxygen demand. There is little romance in a sewage plant, and none in the technicalities of oxygen depletion, thermal stratification or discharge of organic wastes, the destruction of a lake. This is not merely a technical or a political problem. To think of it is to think of all America, of our love-hate relationship with our technology, about our ambivalence about who we are and what we are, about the Hudson and the Missouri, about the Santa Barbara Channel and nuclear bombs, about defoliation in Vietnam and DDT-poisoned fish in Michigan, about all the things we value, often in contradiction, in our past and our future, in nature and technology.

As the plane descends over the murky waters along the Cleveland shore, the brown edging the blue, I have to imagine kids I knew, kids like Cokry Divoky, years ago, scanning the skies for hawks and heron or walking the ice

in the winter, and now confronting the public servants of
the draft board and the crusade for freedom in Asia; and
I hear the reminiscences of old men, telling fish stories
about walleye and whitefish and blue pike, species that
have all but disappeared. How much, you ask, setting
down at Hopkins Airport, is this worth; how much is
romance and sentimentality about a fading past, how
much the price of progress, how much the comfortable
guilt of safe men who can attack pollution as an indis-
putable evil (or war, or technology itself) while languish-
ing in their benefits?

Some thirteen million people live in the basin of this
lake, 90 percent of them on the American side, the rest
in Ontario, the polluters and the polluted, perpetrators
and victims, all of them dependent on a body of water
which, according to the best evidence, is not yet dead but
in danger. They drink its water, swim on its beaches, eat
its fish, and sail from its harbors. Each day at the same
time they, their cities, and their factories dump, leak,
pipe or drop into the lake several hundred million pounds
of sewage, chemicals, oil, and detergents, fouling beaches,
killing wildlife and imperiling the water itself. Sometimes
you can smell and taste it as it comes out of the tap,
sometimes you can see it on the beaches and often in the
rivers—the Maumee, the Auglaize, the Ottawa—but most
significantly you fear, not what already exists, but what
might and could happen if the process continues. In parts
of the western end of the lake, the blue-green algae, which
thrive on the excess of nutrients from sewage, turn blue
water to a murky green and accumulate in heavy mounds
on the shore; in Sandusky, once one of the largest fresh-
water ports in the world, a large fishing industry has been
reduced to a couple of operators who truck their low-grade
catch to Georgia (where, apparently, people are still

hungry enough to buy it); and in Cleveland the industrial stream called the Cuyahoga River is pronounced a fire hazard, a declaration that sounded hyperbolic until, last June, the oil on the river began to burn, damaging two bridges. Cleveland's two fireboats travel the river periodically, hosing oil off docks and pilings so that the inflammable ooze will slowly make its way downstream and into the lake. At the same time, a broken city main is dumping twenty-five million gallons of raw sewage into the river each day. Periodically the main is repaired, and now the city, with a $100-million bond issue voted last fall, is preparing to improve collection and treatment for its entire system and for the neighboring communities which it serves. (Cleveland, incidentally, may also be one of the few municipalities in the world that chlorinates its lake front beaches so they will be safe for swimming.) But when it comes to pollution of the lake, Cleveland is more a victim than a culprit. Cleveland fouls its own nest with its dirty river and its inadequate sewage system, while Detroit, which dumps the waste of a huge industrial population into the Detroit River, stocks Lake Erie. Approximately 65 percent of the oxygen-depleting wastes in the lake come from Detroit; 9 percent from Cleveland. "When it comes to polluting the main part of the lake," said a researcher at the U.S. Bureau of Commercial Fisheries, "Cleveland's hardly on the map."

And yet, in a way, everything is on the map. Everything contributes to and suffers from the condition of the lake: people in five states, a Canadian province, and hundreds of towns and cities from Toledo to Buffalo: Akron, Erie, Cleveland, Lorain, Conneaut, Ashtabula. The federal government has identified three hundred sixty sources of industrial waste, which include power plants, steel mills, chemical companies, food processors, rubber companies; during every heavy rain, silt and flooding sewers spill into the lake, and even in normal periods silt and fertilizers and pesticides drain into its tributaries. But the greatest polluters may be the city sewage systems themselves. The federal government has estimated that with existing treatment facilities the cities along the lake discharge effluent equal, in its composition and effects on the lake, to the raw sewage from a population of 4.7 million people. Some cities are providing secondary treatment, some primary, some none at all. Lake Erie has been called a huge cesspool, an appellation that has at least marginal accuracy. What is absolutely accurate is the statement that in the last fifty years pollution has substantially altered the ecology of the lake, and that it has made the lake far older than its years.

The word, among the scientists, is eutrophication, the process of aging. All lakes grow old as they collect runoff and materials from the surrounding shores. Over hundreds of thousands of years they accumulate enough silt from erosion and organic materials eventually to turn them into marshes and, finally, into dry land. In Lake Erie man has accelerated that process with his wastes and sewage. An excess of nutrients, primarily phosphates and nitrates, has produced great growths of algae in the water and impaired the oxygen supply, especially in the deeper water during the summer, and especially at the western end which is hit hardest by the excrement from Detroit. (Biological degrading of the nutrients requires oxygen; when the nutrients are too heavy the oxygen becomes depleted.) Mayflies, which once grew in huge numbers in the western and shallowest end of the lake and which provided a food supply for fish, cisco, blue pike, walleye and other species, have declined; the water has been taken over by sheepshead, carp, and other types that are tolerant of low oxygen conditions and whose eggs can survive the accumulation of sediments at the bottom. Some species which have surmounted changes in food supply and depleted oxygen now take longer to reach maturity. (The total volume of fish caught in the lake each year is as large as ever, but the catch is worth only half of what it was ten years ago; most of the fishing is now done by Canadians.) On occasions there have been duck kills: flight of birds which have landed on oily water and never flew again, either (it is assumed) because the oil destroyed their natural protection against the water, or because they were poisoned. (There has been some serious talk in recent years about oil drilling in the lake; so far the derricks of the Canadian Pacific Oil and Gas Company which have been erected on the Ontario side of the lake are producing only natural gas.) There is also a possibility that the algae, under certain conditions, can manufacture their own poisons, endangering wild life—and possibly human life.

Because the lake is relatively shallow, there is hope that once the rate of pollution is retarded (hopefully, but not certainly, through improved sewage treatment) the lake, with proper oxygen circulation, can recover, spilling its wastes into Lake Ontario and, ultimately, into the Atlantic. The certainty of that recovery, and the effectiveness of the measures now being planned (which, among other things, include the removal of phosphates before effluent is discharged into the lake) is still a matter of debate—and of time. What is not a matter of debate is that in the past fifty years Lake Erie has aged fifteen thousand years.

Barry Commoner, a Washington University (St. Louis) biologist, who has long been concerned with the abuses of technology expressed:

The lake is threatened with death. . . . Since the area was first settled, Lake Erie has been increasingly burdened with organic wastes and with inorganic nutrients that the Lake's algae convert to organic materials. These organic materials would long ago have asphyxiated most of the Lake's living things had it not been for the peculiar power of iron III [an iron compound called ferric iron] to form insoluble complexes with the materials of the bottom mud. The protective skin of iron III has held the enormous accumulation of potential oxygen demanding material in the muddy bottom of the lake. But this protective skin can remain intact only so long as there is sufficient oxygen present in the water over the mud. For many years this was so, and the layer of iron III held the accumulating mud materials out of the lake water. But a serious oxygen depletion now occurs in the summer months. As a result the protective layer of iron III has begun to break down—exposing the lake to heavy impact of the accumulated algal nutrient long stored in the mud. If the process continues, we may face a sudden biological cataclysm that will exhaust, for a time, most of the oxygen in the greater part of the lake water. Such a catastrophe would make the lake's present difficulties seem slight by comparison.

The fear is that under existing conditions Erie could, without warning, turn into a huge swamp. Among the officials of the Federal Water Pollution Control Administration (FWPCA), which is charged with enforcing pollution-control measures, Commoner is regarded as a prophet of gloom, a Cassandra who is trying to frighten people. Nonetheless, FWPCA paraphrased Commoner's statement in its own report on the lake. "Some of that," said one FWPCA official, "was a little exaggerated. We know that the iron III tends to break down and to release nutrients from the bottom, but there hasn't been any cataclysm, and there's not going to be one."

And yet, perhaps, that's not the issue, shouldn't be the

issue. The trouble with conservation is that it has always been a matter of calamities and cataclysms. In the confusion of state, local, and federal anti-pollution responsibilities, there is always a large measure of sympathy for the company or the city that has to spend money for better treatment facilities, for the corporate taxpayer who might move somewhere else, for the time it takes, for the problems involved. The questions are thus always questions of resources, of priorities, of urgency and time. How much are fish worth? What's the value of a duck? What is the relationship between defoliants in Vietnam (or the price of automobiles in Detroit) and an acid discharge on the Cuyahoga or the Maumee? If a major steel company can increase its earnings $60 million a year by raising the price of steel, then is the expenditure of $18 million for new waste-treatment facilities at its plant in Cleveland something to brag about? How much passion and effort are required by the hypothetical impairment of a municipal water supply? ("The time's going to come," said an angry conservationist in Cleveland, "when they won't be able to put any more chlorine into the drinking water. What the hell are they going to do then?") And to what extent is water or air pollution a problem that only the comfortable can afford? The kids from Cleveland's Hough ghetto (and many others) rarely worry about swimming from polluted beaches; for them and their parents, urban pollution has other, more virulent forms. Their problem, among other things, is rats, not fish.

In the meantime, life on the lake goes on. In most places the problem is invisible; in others it becomes part of the background, an element of lore, like a volcanic mountain on a South Sea island. "People come here expecting to see a swamp," said a Cleveland newspaper reporter. "But there isn't any." On the west side of Catawba Island, near

Sandusky, the cabin cruisers and the yawls luxuriate in their elegant marinas, and on the northern tip the Chevvies back their trailer-borne runabouts onto concrete ramps for a few hours of fishing or a cruise to Put In Bay. At Huntington Park, just west of Cleveland, a kid pinches his toe on the beach and asks whether there's a species of crab that lives only in polluted water, and in Sandusky, Tony DeMore, one of the few remaining commercial fish operators on the American side stands on his wharf and complains that the problem isn't pollution but overfishing and inequitable regulations that permit Canadians to haul what Americans have to throw back. "Now they're stocking the lake with Coho salmon like they did Lake Michigan to bring the sport fishermen back, but they're driving out the small fish. If Lake Erie had been meant for big fish the big fellow up there would have put 'em in. It wasn't pollution that drove the fish out. It was . . . nature. If somebody doesn't pull the Coho out, they'll take over the lake." On the Cuyahoga River, twice each day, the excursion boat *Goodtime II* takes tourists on a run of the industrial sites; a tape-recorded spiel piped over *Goodtime*'s loudspeakers describes the adjacent activities of the Great Lakes Towing Company, U.S. Steel, Republic Steel, Sherwin-Williams Paint, National Sugar Refining and Standard Oil. (No word about waste discharges, about the phenols and oils and acids that ooze into the river. "If you fall in," they say along the river, "you won't drown, you'll decay.") At the foot of the river, on the flats off Front Street, the customers of Fagan's Beacon House sit at their tables just above the ooze listening to Dixieland on summer evenings, drinking beer, and watching the ships go by: it is, they say in Cleveland, one of the places Where Everybody Goes.

The lake is a presence, a landmark, an opening in the

undifferentiated Midwestern landscape, a hole in the
world. Every day the ships come through the Seaway—the
French, the Swedes, the Norwegians—unloading their
cargoes on the city piers. In Vermillion, the lagoon, despite
its murky surface, its oil slicks and its junk, becomes a
backdoor roadway to space; you tie your boat to the cleats
in the backyard and take the folks on a Sunday cruise; and
in Sandusky an octogenarian Negro sits on a pier with
one of his twenty-one children casting for sheepshead or
carp or whatever cares to bite. (The lake is not large, yet
large enough to be infinite. It offers its lore of ships and
waves and weather, the summer storms that drift across
the water, driving the waves into the narrow beaches,
perpetuating sailor stories and seaside quarrels about
which can be worse, the lakes or the Atlantic. And thus
there are legendary events and records of disaster: huge
steamboats that went down in flames, taking their immigrant passengers with them, Commodore Perry in 1814,
Indians in their silent canoes.) The lake is life: Euclid
Beach and Cedar Point, Catawba and Sandusky Bay,
amusement parks, boats for hire, elegant summer houses
tree-shielded from the curious roadway, beach-club privacy, and breakwaters spiny with the antennae of fishing
poles. The beer cans collect between the rocks of the
jetties, and behind them ragged rubber tires, twigs, and
oily cartons undulate against the stones. *A Clean Beach
is a Fun Beach* (posted), two hundred yards from the
city's own outfall of sewage. "Why can't we have swimming in Lake Erie?" the mayor asks his commissioner of
public utilities, and so the water around the beaches is
fenced in with heavy sheets of Dacron anchored to the
bottom, the chlorine is piped in, and the black workmen
rake the accumulated algae into little piles. On July 4 the
beach is dedicated to safe swimming. "I have this vision,"

says a smart mouth. "The mayor arrives in a helicopter and climbs down a rope ladder onto the algae while the Cleveland Orchestra plays 'Shifting Sands.'"

Who controls this environment? Whose rights are invested in it? The mayor—in this case Carl B. Stokes of Cleveland—is accused of being more interested in creating an image through waterfront chlorination projects than in attacking the fundamental problems. After the Cuyahoga fire, he begins legal action to make the state enforce its own anti-pollution standards against the industries on the river (and perhaps to put a little pressure on the corporate managers); the state, in turn, accuses the mayor and city of lagging behind in their own anti-pollution efforts: "It is obvious," said an official of the Ohio Health Department, "that Cleveland itself is a major contributor to the problems of the Cuyahoga River and that a major cleanup cannot be accomplished until the city corrects its own faults." All the states claim that their industries are in compliance with state health and pollution regulations, which simply means that each year they issue a few admonitions, ask the corporations what efforts they propose to make, and let them continue to operate. "All they're doing," someone said in Cleveland, "is licensing the polluters. It seems that it's impossible for anyone to be in violation." (To which the federal people reply that industry is making more progress with waste-treatment facilities than the cities.)

The buck is supposed to stop at the federally conducted enforcement conferences. Under the club of federal authority, all the states in the lake region—Indiana, Ohio, Michigan, New York, and Pennsylvania—have committed themselves to upgrading their municipal waste-treatment facilities to the point where 80 percent of all phosphates are removed from sewage effluent before it is discharged

into the lake. (Some are already behind on the schedule
and received extensions.) Detroit and Cleveland, among
others, are building new plants and collection facilities,
using local, state, and a little federal money. At the same
time their officers are angry at the paltry federal contribution. While Detroit is scheduled to spend $159 million
and Cleveland has voted its $100-million bond issue for
better treatment and collection, the federal government
spends barely over $200 million a year on pollution re-
search and development for the entire nation. "The federal people are the biggest hypocrites in the bunch," said
a Detroit official. "They go around the country making
speeches; maybe if they made as much noise about getting
us more money as they do about dirt we'd be able to move
a little faster." The reply from Washington: "The people
who are polluting are responsible."

So far the lake has been unaffected, and there is doubt
that even after the scheduled projects are completed they
will be sufficient. In New York State, a Health Department Advisory Committee of scientists was asked the
question: Will phosphate removal retard eutrophication in
Lake Erie? The answer, in words of one syllable: Don't
expect too much. Nonetheless, FWPCA has committed
itself to the process as a necessary first step: phosphates,
which come largely from detergents, say the FWPCA
technicians, are essential to the growth of algae and plank-
ton, so (because it is relatively easy) phosphates will be
removed. No one has yet figured out what to do with the
phosphates once they are precipitated out. They will be
trucked to—where? (Nor is it certain that nitrates, which
flood into the lake from agricultural fertilizers and other
sources, are not major factors in eutrophication. "The scientists can raise all sorts of questions," said Murray Stein,
who is charged with FWPCA's enforcement work. "It

doesn't mean they aren't good questions, but every day's delay in studying means time lost forever. You can only hope." (In Ontario the Water Resources Commission, which has its own problems, speaks about a "break-through" in sewage treatment—a chemical-physical process that is said to remove nutrients more effectively and cheaply than existing methods. But the process, so far, has only been tried under experimental, not operational conditions.) The FWPCA has estimated that it will cost $1.1 billion in pollution-control projects to arrest the process of eutrophication in the next twenty years. Some critics believe the figure is far too low, and a few believe that the job is already impossible, that the lake may already be too far gone.

Who controls this environment? Whose rights are affected, whose life? The issue of pollution creates its own bureaucracies, its own inertia, its own zones of indistinct responsibility. Even though there are federal laws dating back to 1899 which prohibit dumping of oil and refuse into navigable waters, even though the various states have established their own regulations, there has never been—in the memory of federal officials—one suit or one criminal proceeding against a polluter. "Pollution law is a little like anti-trust law," a federal official tells you. "It's hard to establish a connection between discharges and damage." *Whose rights are affected, whose environment is it?* "Every year there's more talk," says David Blaushild, a Cleveland automobile dealer who heads a group called Citizens for Clean Air and Water. "The governor and the mayor come to the conferences and make speeches, and go home, and the pollution goes on. You don't have to study any more. You can smell and see it. It's time to file law suits. Why should people take this crap?" *Does the individual have a constitutional right to clean air and water?* "It's going to take a disaster to wake people up," Blaushild says. "If this generation doesn't do it, the next generation won't know any better. They'll think that swimming in filth is the normal thing to do; they'll think the moon is supposed to be yellow. They'll think they're breathing clean air and drinking clean water because they won't know any better." Blaushild writes the Cleveland science museums to ask why they don't take a stronger position against industrial polluters. (Among their trustees are directors of several local corporations.) One of them answers that Blaushild, by selling Detroit's monoxide machines, has his own share of responsibility. *Who controls this environment?*

Pollution, pesticides, fallout. The world's experience with nuclear tests has begun to create a wholly new concept of civility and community. In a strange way pollution became a problem by analogy: we learned, for example, that the same ecological processes which concentrate strontium-90 in bones concentrate DDT in fish, that contamination in one place jeopardizes life in others. A bomb test in New Mexico kills infants in Mississippi and Alabama; pesticides in Michigan farms poison fish in distant lakes; sewage from Detroit fouls beaches in Ohio. One can respond cheaply by lamenting the fix that science and technology have gotten us into, but a bumper sticker proclaiming SAVE LAKE ERIE pasted barely a foot above a smoky automobile exhaust is more an illustration of the problem than a solution. The burden of moral compromise symbolized by Hiroshima and Nagasaki will not be lifted by building a new sewer system in Detroit, however necessary that system may be: technological amelioration of one facet of environmental destruction can be no more than a surrogate for continued acceptance of its larger and more catastrophic forms. Can one take seriously an organization whose interest in conserving fish is unmatched by a position on the ABM?

The questions are backward: How much civility can we afford after we have paid for Vietnam, for the car, for our missiles? Can we sustain a decent welfare program, despite the war? Can we clean the river without jeopardizing the profits of the steel companies? Because we are trying to satisfy a new and still-unclear sense of community with old priorities, evasion is inevitable. Which is to say that a professed commitment to protect an environment which ends with a squabble over sewer taxes is no commitment at all. The issue of pollution can produce a paranoid fanaticism just like every other; no one has died from swimming on a contaminated beach on Lake Erie or from drinking its water. Yet somehow, if we cannot distinguish between fanaticism on behalf of a distant generation and that which defends immediate returns and private ends, we have simply lost our claim to live.

> The environment [wrote Commoner in *Science and Survival*] is a complex, subtly balanced system, and it is this integrated whole which receives the impact of all the separate insults inflicted by pollutants. Never before in the history of this planet has its thin life-supporting surface been subjected to such diverse, novel and potent agents. I believe that the cumulative effects of these pollutants, their interactions and amplification, can be fatal to the complex fabric of the biosphere. And because man is, after all, dependent on part of this system, I believe that continued pollution of the earth, if unchecked, will eventually destroy the fitness of this planet as a place for human life.

If the greatest thing since the creation was worth twenty-four billion clams, how much is the creation worth?

[1969]

APPALACHIA: AGAIN THE FORGOTTEN LAND

Once again Appalachia is becoming America's forgotten place. Seven years and more than seven billion federal dollars after John F. Kennedy brought the region to national attention, grand solutions have soured into new problems, the exploitation of land and people continues, and even the best and most hopeful efforts are jeopardized by a war ten thousand miles away and by ugly political machines all too close to home.

Because of the work of a handful of dedicated people—VISTA workers, Appalachian volunteers, and local residents—some hope has returned with the mounting welfare checks, and some sense of the possible is growing even in the most remote creeks and hollows. But now the programs that have been most effective, many of them aimed at giving the poor a measure of choice and control, are threatened by the politicians' response to local commercial pressures and by the rapacious demands of the strip-mine operators. Efforts at regional development are being directed by distant planners and small-town chambers of commerce, while individuals trying to organize the poor are called agitators and communists, and are driven from the region under agreements between state politicians and national poverty officials who have become politically too weak to resist.

Appalachia, the original American frontier, extends from southern Pennsylvania to northern Alabama, covering 182,000 square miles of land rich in coal, timber, sandstone, natural gas, water, and some of the most magnificent scenery on the continent. In 1966 nearly a hundred million tons of coal worth close to $400 million were mined in Kentucky alone. Where the strip mines have spared the hillsides, the folded mountains, covered by white oak, pine, walnut, beech, and other trees, extend in all directions to the blue-gray horizon. But in the half-abandoned coal camps that adjoin the sulphur-polluted creeks, on the streets of the little towns, and in the welfare offices, the poverty of the people stands in brutal contrast to the wealth of the land. Along the winding roads the rotting carcasses of abandoned automobiles lie alongside smoldering coal dumps and the decaying tipples of exhausted mines, and in the brown and yellow streams, once rich with fish, the sad trash of poverty accumulates in rusty piles. Appalachia, now growing its third welfare generation, has counties where more than a third of the population is unemployed, where the government check—social

security, welfare, aid to dependent children—is the prime
source of income, and where some men are so far from
their last job that it cannot properly be said that they have
a trade at all. Here the average adult has a sixth-grade
education, three fourths of the children who start school
drop out before they complete the twelfth grade, and the
statistics of human pathology—tuberculosis, silicosis, in-
fant mortality—are so high that they do not belong in the
Western world at all.

Everything has eroded: the best of the resources flow
forever downstream, and toward the industrial cities of
the North. Heavy rains wash the topsoil from the hills and
turn the rivers into muddy torrents, the coal fires the mills
of the North and the generators of the TVA (which is the
prime buyer of Appalachian fuel) while the most skilled
and ambitious of the young leave the hills and hollows to
find work in Cleveland, Chicago, or Detroit. "We've been
the great pool of manpower for the Northeast," said a
poverty worker in eastern Tennessee. "And the pool has
been turned on and off at will. The rest of the country gets
automobiles and the gadgets of affluence. All this region
gets is silicosis."

Appalachia's coal regions enjoyed a brief, uncertain
moment of prosperity during and immediately after World
War II when the war economy and the pressure of John
L. Lewis's United Mine Workers brought decent wages,
hospitals, and pension plans. But when the war boom
ended, many of the mines closed, leaving the survivors
of a single-product economy without resources or useful
skills. The coal industry ultimately returned to prosperity
with a rising demand for fuel, but it did so as a highly
efficient, mechanized enterprise. Using modern equipment, 140,000 men can now dig more coal than 700,000
did twenty years ago. And while many of the deep mines

continue to operate, frequently under enlightened management, a substantial part of the industry is now stripping the mountains, cutting or blasting away the top soil and vegetation, which spills down the slopes, to get at the coal beneath. Each year, at the current rate, the strip mines of Kentucky scar some twelve thousand acres of land, leaving the bare cliffs of the high wall above, and the sliding spoil banks on the hills below.

The legal basis for this damage rests in the so-called broad-form deed: Before strip mining became prevalent, thousands of mountaineers sold their mineral rights to coal and land companies for a few cents an acre, entitling the companies to remove minerals and holding them harmless for any damage except that incurred through malice. The courts have held that this immunity extends even to the uprooting of graves and the destruction of the homes and gardens that are occasionally covered by slides. Under the broad-form deed, said a mountaineer, "they've dug up the dead and buried the living." Although several states have enacted strip mine laws requiring operators to restore the land, and although many companies are diligently trying to comply, enforcement is often difficult or ineffective. In West Virginia, a new statute now entitles property owners to collect triple damages from the coal companies, but in the mountains of eastern Kentucky, that state's law has had little effect. Kentucky's new governor, Louie B. Nunn, received support from the strip-mine interests in the 1967 election, and it is unlikely that he will be overzealous in enforcing or strengthening it. Under his predecessor, Edward T. Breathitt, state officials experimented with techniques of restoring the hillsides, but even they admitted privately that where the slopes are steep, there is no possible way of eliminating slides and reclaiming the land. In the mountains of eastern Kentucky, the only effective hope for conservation appears to be the elimination of the strip mine altogether. (On December 11, 1967, the day Breathitt's term expired, he approved a set of tough regulations, limiting strip mines to slopes of less than 28 degrees; if those regulations stand, they will severely restrict strip mining and will represent a major victory for conservation in the region.)

In this sad economy of food stamps and subsistence, the coal company is no longer the great employer and hence the paternalistic provider it once used to be. Gone are the days when the company owned the buildings, ran the store, and furnished the services, and even the most naïve have now abandoned the hope that some day "the mines will open up again." What remains is the condition of dependency: through a half century of rural industrialization, the once-independent mountaineer was reduced to reliance on a single enterprise, and when it no longer required his labor, to nothing except the dole. The public payroll, and most notably the public schools, now furnish the prime source of employment. In Appalachia, schools mean jobs for bus drivers, clerks, lunchroom employees, coaches, and teachers, and hence they represent the most important source of political power at hand. In the isolated mountain counties, where kinship and tribal loyalties overshadow the abstractions of political ethics, the school superintendent is often a political boss who controls contracts for insurance, construction, and fuel, appointment to other offices, and employment in the system: In Breathitt County, Kentucky, for example, Marie Turner or her husband have held the school superintendency for more than forty years, and hence they also control most of the other offices the county has to offer. There are similar machines in other areas, and although many people feel that people like the Turners have been benevolent bosses—Breathitt County, someone said, would have fallen apart without the Turners—they have been bosses nevertheless. At a time when Appalachia was out of the national consciousness and the mountaineer was a figure for mythology and amusement, the Turners did what they could for their people. The *quid pro quo* was patronage and power.

The American romance with the happy hillbilly came to an end in the early sixties. Prompted by Kennedy's concern with Appalachian poverty, which he saw at first hand in the 1960 West Virginia primary, Americans began to discover the misery behind the moonshine. Television crews and magazine writers swarmed to the hills in such numbers that one Kentucky motel owner began to conduct photographic safaris to hollows that he promised "ain't been worked yet." While bands of hungry, desperate miners roamed the coal regions dynamiting trains and bridges, Congress passed the Manpower Development and Training Act, the Appalachia Redevelopment Act, and a variety of other measures designed to bring the heretofore invisible poor some share of the affluence that most Americans took for granted. Although the federal poverty program was aimed at all indigent Americans, Appalachia came to symbolize, along with the urban ghetto, the most pressing item on the nation's social agenda. As a consequence, special funds were appropriated for the construction of Appalachian highways, water facilities, and hospitals; the distribution of surplus food was augmented through a food-stamp program which enables the poor to purchase more groceries than their welfare checks would otherwise permit; unemployed fathers have been given jobs, at $1.25 an hour, in a "work experience and training" program (they are generally called happy pappies); young men and women have been enrolled in the Job Corps and the

Neighborhood Youth Corps; vocational education has received increased support, and large sums have been made available for the education of the disadvantaged, which, in the mountain counties, means almost everybody.

To anyone visiting Appalachia now, these programs have clearly had an effect: new roads and vocational schools are under construction or already in use; the happy pappies have planted trees on hillsides that had been covered by strip-mine spoil banks; medical facilities are more accessible; the school dropout rate has been reduced (partly because federal funds are keyed to enrollment); and there appear to be fewer obvious signs of malnutrition than there were three years ago. In some families the money earned by adolescents in the Youth Corps has become the most important source of income. It has also become a source of pride and respect: "After those kids received their first pay check," said Don Roarke, the director of a four-county Youth Corps in eastern Kentucky, "they were dressed better, they held their heads higher. You could see the difference." At the same time, the graduates of many vocational programs are finding jobs as heavy-machine operators and mine technicians, a few of them in the mountains, others in Northern cities.

For many more, however, the existing programs serve only to hide the misery: the new highways are beginning to make it possible to cross large portions of Appalachia without seeing a tar-paper shack or a coal dump; the food stamps run out before the end of the month, and the schools, though far better than they used to be, still remain a blind alley, graduating kids who are approximately two years behind the national average on standardized tests. "The bare gut essentials are now being met," said Tom Gish, the editor of the Whitesburg (Kentucky) *Mountain Eagle,* who is undoubtedly the most outspoken and dedicated journalist in the region. "By and large people are getting fed and getting coal for the winter. If you go back to the early sixties when there was mass hunger and violence, then you can say there's been improvement. Peace has been restored."

But the peace is shaky, and the economy remains dependent on the federal government. President Johnson's declaration that "the dole is dead" was, to say it mildly, premature. Poverty remains endemic: median family income in eastern Kentucky is $2,080, and Gish predicts that if poverty funds are reduced there will be more violence. In the county seats the prosperous get roads and water lines and sewers, but only a few miles away, the privies stand alongside the dirty creeks from which people draw their water, rain turns the unpaved roads into muddy ruts, and the kids can't go to school because they have no shoes.

The prime beneficiaries of government funds appear to be the swelling banks, which are afraid to invest their deposits in anything but government bonds, the small businesses, and the politicians. For all their ignorance and isolation the economic and political interests of Appalachia have a highly developed knack for using outside help to perpetuate the existing structure and the conditions of dependency. In Perry County, Kentucky, a political enemy of a former county school superintendent used his influence as director of a Youth Corps project to help elect a new school board and oust the superintendent; the new administration then rewarded him with the directorship of another federally financed program administered by the schools. In other areas, the directors of happy-pappy programs discourage their charges from participating in community-action groups that threaten local political machines, and in almost every community the traditions of nepotism are so powerful that many people still regard the poverty program as a source of employment rather than as a means of upgrading the skills of human beings and the social health of the community. "Jobs are coveted so much, and loyalties to kin are so strong," said a poverty worker in Kentucky, "that it's pretty hard to persuade anyone that you have to pick people on merit." Although some training programs have brought new skills and confidence, and although many children who had once gone hungry through the school day are now receiving hot lunches (sometimes even in the most remote one-room schools), many school officials have refused to appoint outsiders, preferring the promotion of politically faithful employees to the uncertainties of new blood and new ideas. In one community a group of men who were enrolled for training in construction and maintenance composed a letter to Washington:

> We were in the building and maintainence class under MDTA that took up on April 10 and ended September 29. They told us each day we would have 2 hours of electricity, pluming, carpentry and painting but for the most of it all we did was paint school buildings and repair and cover the roofs of the schools. When some of the men bucked on painting so much they were told if they didnt like it they could leave. To start we was told the government would buy around a thousand dollars of lumber a month for us to work with we unloaded plenty new lumber and racked it up on the racks. For awhile we used some then we was told we could buy it for 25 cents a foot and then they said it wasnt for sale but it still got missing. In electricity all we had were 9 days, on our certificate of training it says we got 320 hours. They just didnt care much if we learned a thing or not we was just putting in time. Now we are in worse shape than when we started and we got knocked off the food stamps for 30 days. We

didnt get the training they said or the permanent jobs they promised at the start. The only jobs we have heard about are temporary and a long way off. A man with a family in school cant just leave out at the promise of a job.

Given these conditions, the most promising idea for Appalachia has been community action—training individuals to organize local groups for social improvement, community welfare, and self-help. As originally conceived, the Community Action Program (CAP) of the Office of Economic Opportunity was to include "maximum feasible participation" of the poor: community-action agencies were, if possible, to be free from domination by local politicians. In some areas of Appalachia the program worked effectively, despite the suspicions of county officials: community centers have been built, small marketing cooperatives (selling quilts and other local products) have been organized, and new leadership has developed. In the eastern Kentucky counties of Leslie, Knott, Letcher, and Perry, a four-county Community Action Program (LKLP), which includes poor people as well as sympathetic county judges, has established a network of depots to inform people of their welfare rights, of new training programs, and of the availability of medical facilities. Among other things, LKLP operated a transportation system to bring the sick from the hollows to the area clinics; it is training local people in welfare work and social service; and it has prompted a number of projects to clear the region of decaying bridges and abandoned coal tipples.

Despite such successes, however—and there are others—many CAP agencies have been captured by established interests or abandoned after local battles destroyed embryonic organizations before they had a chance to function. Many of those that survive must straddle an uncertain line between ineffectiveness and the dangerous course of challenging the established order: Recent congressional action, moreover, indicates that control of all local CAP agencies will be given to local elected officials, thus making CAP, in Appalachia at least, the biggest potential pork barrel since the invention of rivers and harbors.

Because of the limitations of the Community Action Program, some of the most effective community work has been done by VISTA (Volunteers in Service to America, the domestic Peace Corps), by the Appalachian Committee to Save the Land and People, which has been fighting the strip mine, by the long-standing Council of the Southern Mountains, and by the Appalachian Volunteers, a private organization which originated among students at Berea College but which is now fully autonomous. Originally the Appalachian Volunteers (AVs) concentrated on the repair of schoolhouses, the distribution of books—more than one million were collected and placed in mountain schools—and on other community work. The AVs and VISTAs, who often work together, have moved into isolated mountain communities (places named Marrowbone and Cave Ridge, Clover Fork, and Horse Creek), have come to know the inhabitants, and are helping to create new organizations and a new sense of confidence: adult education groups, nursery schools, community centers, craft shops and, most significantly, a belief that choices are available and collective action possible. "These are the first people," said a woman in the mountains, "who promised to do something, and then did."

What they have done, among other things, is to arouse the suspicions and fears of the established interests. In the past year, the AVs have become increasingly involved in the strip-mine issue and in tax reform, helping to organize protests, transport people to meetings, and warn affected property owners when the strip-mine bulldozers were coming. In their zealousness, some have talked, none too privately, about overturning local political structures and establishing some vague new order. (A few were poorly trained or offensive in dress or manners.) As a consequence, they have been labeled communists and agitators (though many are natives of the region), and they are now threatened with the suspension of all federal support. The precipitating incident took place in the summer of 1967, when a small Pike County (Kentucky) farmer named Jink Ray, supported by his neighbors (and, later, by Appalachian Volunteers), stood in front of the bulldozers of the Puritan Coal Company which had come to strip his land. Within a few days the matter had become a regional cause célèbre and threatened to develop into a mountain shootout. Under the new Kentucky strip-mine law, Governor Breathitt lifted the company's permit, ordering the state's Department of Natural Resources to determine whether the slopes to be mined exceeded the statutory limits. Two weeks later, after several conferences among Pike County officials, the county sheriff, in a midnight raid, arrested an AV field worker named Joe Mulloy and two organizers for the Southern Conference Education Fund on charges of violating a Kentucky sedition law. (The man charged with the prosecution was a former president of the Independent Coal Operators Association who was then a candidate for state office.) In indicting the three, the Pike County grand jury concluded "that a well-organized and well-financed effort is being made to promote and spread the communistic theory of the violent and forceful overthrow of the government of Pike County" and "that the employees of the Appalachian Volunteers and other federally financed antipoverty programs have collaborated and cooperated with known communist organizers to help them organize and promote the violent overthrow of the constitutional government of Pike County." The grand jury, said Harry M. Caudill, the Whitesburg attorney who is probably the most eloquent spokesman for the mountains, "was certain that the revolution was about to begin in Pike County, and that the neighboring counties, in domino fashion, would then fall to the enemy."

Although the sedition law was quickly declared unconstitutional by a federal court, the Pike County affair reinforced suspicions not only about the Appalachian Volunteers, but about everything that smacked of community action. In many eastern Kentucky counties VISTA workers are no longer welcome. In West Virginia, Governor Hulett Smith, while praising the VISTA program in mental health, charged the AVs with "misconduct" and demanded an Office of Economic Opportunity investigation. In Kentucky, Governor Breathitt (who could not succeed himself as governor but was nonetheless involved in the political campaign) demanded and received assurances from OEO Director Sargent Shriver that some current OEO grants to the Appalachian Volunteers would not be renewed, and that the cancellation of other federal support for AV activities would receive "most serious consideration." In Hazard, Kentucky, a few months later, an exasperated staff member of the Community Action Agency declared, "We're still trying to beat this Red rap. People in the Work Experience and Training Program have been told that if they had anything to do with us they'd be off the rolls."

What is most in jeopardy now is not merely the budget of the Appalachian Volunteers (who are trying to find private funds to replace their uncertain federal support), but the principle of independent community action itself.

The efforts of the past three years have (in some areas at least) generated a degree of independence that will be difficult to arrest: even before the poverty program began, the Appalachian Group to Save the Land and People, composed entirely of mountaineers, had begun to campaign for stricter strip-mine laws and for the imposition of a severance tax on the minerals that now flow untaxed from the region. In the creeks and hollows, residents have stopped bulldozers, sometimes with their bodies, sometimes with shotguns and dynamite. When Youth Corps funds ran out during the 1967 congressional debate on the poverty program, the staff members in many Appalachian communities came to work anyway, and when Shriver announced the curtailment of AV support, the residents of a number of mountain communities signed letters and telegrams of protest. This fall, for the first time in history, teachers in an eastern Kentucky county went on strike for higher pay. Nevertheless, if prime responsibility for the Appalachian portion of the war on poverty is delegated to the established regimes, the basic political arrangements will remain unchanged: every dollar in federal funds will make the politicians that much stronger.

And yet, even if Appalachia's poor achieve greater political power and independence, the problems will persist. "You can't have real community action," said a Kentucky CAP director, "until you have economic choice." To date, regional development has meant a few highways and hospitals, not jobs. The area's topography and its unskilled population make it unattractive to industry, and have led to the desperate suggestion that the best program is training people so they can move away. "They want to regard these towns as breeding grounds," said Robert Cornett, who was Breathitt's director of area development. "I'm

losing faith in the planners. They're always looking for
big solutions. You have to do it slowly with roads and
health and small businesses, woodworking industries or
maybe poultry." People like Cornett hope to encourage
the construction of new housing (which is desperately
needed) through the pooling of public and private resources and to foster greater local concern for development. "You have to use what's here, to improve the power
structure, not tear it down." So far, the results have been
meager. In some of the county seats, even the most proper
people are still unpersuaded that poverty really exists, or
that it would persist if the unemployed just had enough
character to work. "I grew up here in Hazard," said a staff
member at the local CAP, "but I never noticed the poverty
until I went outside. I never saw it."

Perhaps the chief consequence of the recent programs
in Appalachia is the realization that poverty and exploitation, isolation and ignorance, are not susceptible to left-
handed solutions, that they are linked to the general
affluence, and that they raise moral questions which strike
at the very heart of America's willingness to bring a decent
life to all its citizens. What do the Combs and Caudills,
the Napiers and Brashears, of eastern Kentucky think after
the food stamps run out in the third week of the month,
and they hear the President declare that the "dole is
dead"? What kind of judgment does one make about a
nation that can spend close to $500,000 to kill a Viet Cong
but less than $150 a month to support the family of an
unemployed miner who lives in a place called Stinking
Creek? How great is a society that permits the systematic,
mechanized defacing of its hillsides while it encourages
the natives of these same hills to move into the slums of
Detroit? "People expected this thing solved in six months,"

said Perley F. Ayer, the chairman of the Council of the Southern Mountains. "But in education alone we're five million years behind."

It is difficult to cheer the results of Appalachian development or the war on poverty: the harmonious interplay of poverty, politics, and the welfare mind combine to frustrate even the most valiant effort. But it is even more difficult to criticize the intent of these programs or the officials who are charged with running them. They have been forced to live with a limited and reluctant mandate that prohibits them from anything more than making poverty bearable and, if possible, invisible. The vested Appalachian interests in the status quo—coal companies, railroads, banks, local bar associations, insurance agencies, politicians—are so vast that they represent a fair cross-section of American society itself. Their stockholders and beneficiaries live all over the nation; they help sustain our affluence. If Appalachia hasn't changed, it may be in part because too many are dependent on it as it is. "The reason little has happened," said Ayer, "is that America doesn't have its heart in it."

[1967]

THE FOUR-YEAR GENERATION

Lyndon B. Johnson will be remembered as the man who tried to turn the clock back four years and failed. Johnson's self-immolation, his announcement that he will not accept his party's nomination for another term of office, was so unexpected that it left the network commentators speechless and the experts stuttering. Yet there was one unmistakable suggestion in the speech: his warnings of divisiveness in America were strongly reminiscent of the remarks he made about extremism after the assassination of John F. Kennedy. The President was offering his political corpse to the national cause, was trying to use his own demise much as he was able to use Kennedy's—to rally the nation to a new sense of common purpose. In courting the hand of history, he may well have begun the end of the Vietnam war. But in trying to reestablish the mood of 1964, he failed, because the intervening four years have become an insurmountable barrier between the past and the present.

Lyndon Johnson did not create that barrier. Nor is it merely a product of the accumulating political and moral excrescences of Vietnam. The war has undoubtedly extracted a fearful price in frustrated domestic reform, curtailed programs, and social revulsion; it helped destroy the optimism that stimulated Johnson's successes with medicare, civil rights, federal aid to education, and the war on poverty (and which, in turn, helped feed the optimism); and it certainly divided the country, not only between hawks and doves but between people and government. For many, the credibility gap has become as large as all alienation. Yet, oddly enough, the real divisions in contemporary Amercian society would probably have occurred anyway, and the gulf between 1964 and the present might have been as large even if Vietnam had never happened. Vietnam may or may not be unique among American wars in its technological and impersonal brutality; but it was certainly the first war whose viciousness was so thoroughly documented by television. It helped accelerate changes that were inevitable; Vietnam, as Dick Gregory has said, exposed America to America.

In a peculiar way, both Johnson and the war have been unifying forces. Without them there would have been even less common ground between (for example) middle-class liberals, the Old Left, the radicals of the New Left, and the traditional pacifists. Out of the ooze of consensus politics, Vietnam created a new community of dissent.

Johnson represented a lightning rod, and the war a platform around which the critics could rally. If both disappear, the various liberal elements in America may be
left running about like the survivors of an ant hill newly
destroyed by an uncomprehended foot. Some of this is
already apparent in the divisions among McCarthy, Kennedy, and Humphrey, in the sudden shift of roles that
Johnson's withdrawal thrust upon each, and in the state
of uncertainty that the Vietnam peace flirtations left the
doves. It has become even more apparent in the failure
of liberalism to muster sufficient pressure on Congress
for major new poverty or welfare legislation, despite the
murder of Martin Luther King and the emphatic warnings
of the report of the U.S. Commission on Civil Disorders.
Lyndon Johnson's announcement immediately after King's
murder that he would go to a joint session of Congress
to ask for new legislation has not been mentioned since
the day his promised appearance was "temporarily post-
poned."

There is divisiveness in America, but its roots go deeper
than the Vietnam war. The fact is that American liberalism has been separated from its traditional constituents,
divided in its ranks, and derailed by its own achievements.
Among the greatest opponents of integration are the
lower-class white minorities of the cities (the Poles of
Chicago, the Irish of South Boston), groups that belonged
to the great coalition forged by Franklin Roosevelt thirty
years ago; the most restricted organizations are not colleges and country clubs, but the building trades unions;
the most alienated and fearful Americans are not blacks,
but urban whites, who are buying guns and police dogs
against the black revolution they believe is imminent.
More important, our faith in painless temporary programs
—for curing poverty or integrating Negroes—has proved

excessive, if not downright naïve, and our programs against social inequity and injustice have been fractured, clouded, and challenged by the growing realization that most Americans have a personal stake in the very inequities they always professed to deplore. The Riot Commission confronted those who read its report with an unqualified description of white racism and with a warning that we are all culpable and will all have to pay if America is not to be permanently split into two unequal societies, one black, one white. It made clear, in the prosaic tones of an Establishment report, that we are living the American dilemma—that we are chained to it.

The big political change of the past four years is that the New Deal has finally come to an end. Johnson's well-intentioned liberalism has turned out to be almost as anachronistic as the Neanderthal Goldwaterism we rejected in 1964. History and tradition had seemed to indicate that through relatively cheap social action we could remedy severe domestic problems, resolve world crises, and rescue nations in the cause of righteousness. Our gray achievements in the war on poverty and our dismal record in Vietnam have indicated simultaneously that history and tradition can sometimes be fearful liars.

Lyndon Johnson, who acted as if Vietnam were Munich and the Great Society the New Deal, has been defeated not only by events but by the growing gap between those events and the social understanding required to confront them. It is not simply that rural congressmen don't understand the problems of the cities or that Main Street lags behind New York, but that the idea of programmatic responses to major problems is itself under challenge for the first time. Until recently we believed that large reforms came in small packages labeled education, health, or housing which could be bought painlessly as funds became available. Acquiring them would not affect (we thought) the privileges of others. In four years of the Great Society, we have begun to discover that the advantages of those who have power and resources are inextricably tied to the disadvantages of those who do not. We learned that it is impossible to maintain suburban homogeneity and integrated communities at the same time, that part of the wealth of New York and Pittsburgh depends on the mining of cheap Appalachian coal and the exploitation of mountaineers, that the wines of California are made with the sweat of migrants, and that it is impossible under existing practices to use schools and colleges as instruments to select some for economic advancement without using the same schools to reject others.

We have learned, moreover, that the intellectuals, who were supposed to devise programs and run the nation on a solid foundation of intelligence, can be just as inept and corruptible as anyone else. Neither Robert McNamara's computers, nor Walt Rostow's economic theories, nor Arthur Schlesinger's liberalism prevented either the moral or the political disasters of Vietnam. Universities and scholars have been among the prime beneficiaries of secret CIA support and Defense Department research contracts. The intellectuals, as Christopher Lasch recently pointed out, have been fascinated by power and conspiracy. "Time after time," he said, "it has been shown that the dream of influencing the war machine is a delusion. Instead the war machine corrupts the intellectuals. The war machine cannot be influenced by the advice of well-meaning intellectuals in the inner councils of government; it can only be resisted. The way to resist it is simply to refuse to put oneself at its service." In some respects, these developments are not surprising: What is significant is that four years ago most people believed otherwise. In the Eisenhower years, the academics shuddered at the President's choice of cronies: businessmen, bankers, golfers. Intellectuals, they felt, could save the nation; they were our last and best resource. The academics who charged Eisenhower with being an innocent were at least as innocent as he was.

So we are in a brand new ball game produced not only by Johnson's withdrawal or even by the compression of time and events but by the seismic tremors of a new mood, a new style, and a new kind of man. The central fact of 1968, it seems to me, is youth. Here I'm not referring to the platform clichés of student uprisings, LSD, sex, hippies, or the Beatles, although they are all part of the scene. I mean, more basically, that perhaps for the first time many Americans are looking to those younger than themselves rather than those who are older. America is bemused by its youth, black and white: look at any newspaper. The news is being made by people under thirty. (I am aware that young men have always been in the vanguard of reform and revolution, but in America, at least, they tended to carry the message and credentials of others—they were doing someone else's thing.) The young—the blacks of the cities, the whites of the suburbs, the college students, and the peaceniks—are looked upon as the initiators and inventors of ferment, change, and rebellion. There are, to be sure, few new faces (and almost no young faces) in the limelight of national politics. *But there are new crowds,* and the crowds, whether peaceful or violent, have given American social action in the last few years its characteristic stamp. Perhaps this is only a consequence of the lack of effective political leadership, but that seems a doubtful proposition. Many of the young radicals (and the hippies and dropouts) are not interested either in history or programs, and have been noted for their monumental apathy toward new pieces of social legislation. What they are looking for is a vague sort of personal engagement, and if they have overused such borrowed phrases as confrontation, those come nearest to expressing what is being asked. In a sense they, like the black militants, have no use for the official history, which is, finally, the history of middle-class liberalism. Whether they will ever begin to try to write their own, as the black nationalists are now doing, or whether they will be satisfied with their historical virginity is uncertain. Yet, like the blacks, they don't want to be part of a program, and don't want to enlist (for very long) in anything that demands personal compromise in the cause of organized large-scale action. The Washington peace demonstration of last fall, as Norman Mailer pointed out, was a collection of disparate elements held together by the genius of David Dellinger, who organized it, but unable to agree on anything but the date of the demonstration.

All this could change, of course. The rootless rebels of other times have become the disciplined storm troops of fascist states; alienation is in itself the most unreliable of conditions, and anarchy can produce not only repression from without but boredom from within. Within the protests the spurious and the shabby co-exist with the genuine and the passionate, and the temptation could always come to junk the one with the other. We have, in our lifetime, seen two McCarthys, and we know that each of them has been able to gain followers and win votes.

The quixotic behavior of many young Americans has been variously explained, generally by moralists of the older generation. What seems to be most applicable (and applicable to many older Americans as well) is the concept of what Robert Jay Lifton in an article in *Partisan Review* has called Protean Man, the individual who is able relatively easily to alter his sense of himself, and to change ideologies "with a new ease that stands in sharp contrast to the inner struggle we have in the past associated with these shifts." "Until relatively recently," Lifton says, "no more than one major ideological shift was likely to occur in a lifetime, and that one would be accompanied by pro- found soul-searching and conflict. But today it is not un- usual to encounter several such shifts accomplished rather painlessly, within a year or even a month; and among many groups, the rarity is a man who has gone through life holding firmly to a single ideological vision."

In Lifton's view, "political and religious movements, as they confront Protean Man, are likely to experience less difficulty convincing him to alter previous convictions than they do providing him with a set of beliefs which can command his allegiance for more than a brief experimental interlude." If this is the case, the politicians are going to require more sensitive antennae; they are also going to find it increasingly difficult to rally continuing support for any complex program. More important, if Lifton is cor- rect (and other evidence seems to bear him out), then we are going to continue to face a new generation, a new mood, a new state of mind, not every twenty-five years or every ten, but every two or three or four. Some of the major polling organizations are already pointing out that opinions can change more rapidly than they can sample them.

The problem is whether a majority of Americans, and the political process itself, can adapt to the ferment that many people feel but often fail to understand. The cities are on the verge of explosion; if they don't explode acci- dentally (that is, if the organized militants can keep things cool), they may well explode in another year when the militants are better organized, have developed a set of specific demands, and can discipline and direct the frustration and violence that ignited spontaneously last summer. In one Northern ghetto, a CORE leader who had worked hard to keep things calm after the murder of Martin Luther King declared that "there's no point in unplanned action. It's nonproductive." He spoke of objectives and demands (among them ghetto control of the local schools and police) "that don't turn off black people" and that can be realized through organized militancy—violent or peaceful, as the need arises. Although such militants represent a minority, they have gained new allies in the black middle class; more important, they have enabled (or even forced) Negro moderates to escalate their demands and to increase their bargaining power with the white establishment. In 1964 no one had ever heard the phrase "Black Power," and most Americans were still vaguely committed to integration. That black nationalists have begun to sit on ghetto reform committees with downtown bankers is a small index of how far the nation has moved in four years.

Nonetheless, the ferment in America is neither all black or all urban. There remain some forty million poor in this nation, the majority of them white, who are not only a burden on the conscience, but who will (sooner or later) begin to learn something from Stokely Carmichael and Rap Brown, even if they never learned it from Marx or Lenin. And immediately above them in the economic scale are uncounted millions of lower-middle-class whites who may well be the most neglected individuals in America: the stevedores and taxi drivers, the followers of George Wallace and Louise Day Hicks; people who join Mayor Daley of Chicago in their willingness to kill or maim looters, and who are deeply resentful of the attention being paid to the Negro while they themselves live in shoddy neighborhoods without decent parks and schools. According to the most reliable estimates, more than half of all American homes contain some kind of fire-arm, and all the evidence indicates that the gun market has been especially strong in the last two years. We are beginning to feel the potential for violence and destruction around us.

Anywhere one goes in America in 1968, there are mani-festations of social sickness and social change, of disloca-tion and reform. In New York City the schoolteachers say they have never seen so many children with emotional problems, and in the suburbs the schools have become trading centers in marijuana. At the same time, the kids are demanding more power of their own, not only in the colleges but in the high schools, and are demonstrating that they can often use it more intelligently than those who reluctantly give it to them.

Alongside sickness there is health: in the Peace Corps and VISTA, in thousands of tutoring programs, in com-munity-service projects, in civil protests. It is another measure of change that activities which were until re-cently considered peculiar or extremist are coming close to being an accepted part of social action: draft resistance grows alongside the general peace movement (in New York, a recent peace march outdrew a competing Loyalty Day parade by a ratio of more than ten to one); sex is no longer un-American, and even the divorce and abortion laws are getting a second look. Suddenly we have a whole generation of young people for whom dissent has become an intellectual and social style. Where until recently people read Marx or C. Wright Mills or Paul Goodman as counterpoint to the conventional wisdom of the textbook and classroom, they are now reading them—and others, such as Herbert Marcuse, Frantz Fanon, and Che Guevara

—as texts. For some of them maturity is not a way into the mainstream, a way of coming to terms with the existing order, but a way out. They are not growing up absurd, but growing up removed and angry.

Certainly these are all minorities: the majority of youngsters are not in active rebellion; most Negroes are not black nationalists; most suburbanites don't smoke pot. But it is a society's minorities that make its revolutions and that define its mainstream. A few hundred black militants have changed, in a few years, the course of race relations in America, and have altered the nature of our consciousness about the problem. The point is simply that the minorities are new; the old divisions of conflict have disappeared. Struggles between capital and labor, between liberals and conservatives, and between Soviet communism and American capitalism have become more rhetorical than real. The discipline and order that those divisions imposed are gone, and we seem to be on the eve of new alignments and new struggles whose nature we can only surmise.

Still, it may be safe to say, for example, that while we may be done with large wars, we are not done with violence in America or anywhere else; that there will be new divisions, not between Russians and Americans but between the developed north of the world and the underdeveloped south, between rich and poor, between the "responsibility" of those who have (food, atom bombs, factories) and the aspirations of those who do not. It may even be possible to say that two thirds of the world, and part of our own society with it, is not only in revolt against colonialism, poverty, and white supremacy, but against the very thing *we* have always called civilization. "When the [African] native hears a speech about Western culture," writes Frantz Fanon in *The Wretched of the Earth,* "he pulls out his knife. . . . The violence with which the supremacy of white values is affirmed and the aggressiveness which has permeated the victory of these values over the ways of life and of thought of the native mean that, in revenge, the native laughs in mockery when Western values are mentioned in front of him. In the colonial context the settler only ends his work of breaking in the native when the latter admits loudly and intelligibly the supremacy of the white man's values." Fanon might well be talking also of some black Americans: in America, they will say, it was the white man who brought violence and who is still its greatest perpetrator. It was always the man who brought a "higher civilization"—whether it was to the blacks of Africa, or to the American Indian, or to the peasants of Vietnam—who was able to be most efficiently brutal and violent. The man too supremely confident of his own civilization and values can also be the most unregenerate of killers.

The question, again, is whether traditional political processes can contain and accommodate the new movements, alliances, and passions without repression or anarchy. The coming political campaign will, knowingly or not, be very much involved with this matter; it will demand a debate not only about immediate political issues but a confrontation of how America thinks of itself and of its stance toward those who, with varying degrees of maturity and responsibility, are issuing demands on its conscience and its purse. Perhaps more than any other, the election of 1968 will have to determine not only the Presidency but the nature of American politics and the stability of American life. How much turbulence can we stand and swallow? How much freedom can this, the most free of political systems, entertain and encourage? To what extent can a competitive, centralized, industrial technology honor the claims of dissident groups who profess a humanity beyond conventional, social and political arrangements? And how, finally, will we be able to distinguish the spurious claims of the rabble-rousers and con artists from genuine beliefs and legitimate demands? How will we know when someone—be he Rap Brown, Ho Chi Minh, or George Wallace—is only putting us on?

To travel through America in 1968 is to travel through a country at war—at war in Vietnam and at war with itself. There, in the planes and bus terminals are the uniformed servicemen and the raw recruits being led off to boot camp; there, in the newspapers of small towns are the reports of local casualties and the lists of new draftees. Next to them are the peace parades, the draft resisters, and the relentless documentation—night after night—of brutality in a distant country of suffering men. And beside them both is the daily round of life in American towns and cities, often still personal, decent, and concerned, and therefore hardly able to comprehend what the tumult is all about. Main Street is sometimes poorly informed, but its decency and good sense have often served as a flywheel to the frenetic impulses of those who know better. That decency and good sense are going to be tested as never before. If we can be certain of anything, it is that normalcy from now on will be change and turbulence, and that domestic tranquility will be the ability to live with them.

"I am aware," wrote de Tocqueville in 1835, "that many of my contemporaries maintain that nations are never their own masters here below, and that they necessarily obey some insurmountable and unintelligent power, arising from anterior events, from their race, or from the soil and climate of their country. Such principles are false and cowardly; such principles can never produce aught but feeble men and pusillanimous nations. Providence has not created mankind entirely independent or entirely free. It is true that around every man a fatal circle is traced beyond which he cannot pass; but within the wide verge of that circle he is powerful and free; as it is with man, so with communities. The nations of our time cannot prevent the conditions of men from becoming equal, but it depends upon themselves whether the principle of equality is to lead them to servitude or freedom, to knowledge or barbarism, to prosperity or wretchedness."

[1968]

FROM CHICAGO TO NOVEMBER

Most political conventions are party exercises composed of varying degrees of strife, hoopla, ritual, and serious debate. They exist to nominate candidates, or to ratify candidates that are already all but nominated. Most are forgotten before the election takes place. The Democratic convention in Chicago, on the other hand, may well prove to be a watershed for the party and perhaps for the nation. It produced no major surprises in the candidates that were nominated; but it revealed and probably reinforced divisions, changes, and disturbances in the very foundations of American political society. There probably hasn't been a convention like Chicago since the Civil War, and there may never be another.

"A lot was lost in Chicago," said a young congressional candidate after the Democratic convention. "I lost my voice, Mayor Daley lost his image, and the Democrats lost the election." In a week of political acrimony, police violence, and, for some, unspeakable rage and frustration, many people lost their voices, their composure, and—in at least a few instances—their party or even their country. "I never knew it could be like this," said a delegate from Wisconsin. "This is unbelievable."

This—the clubbings inflicted by police on demonstrators and bystanders, the capricious harassment called "security" at the International Amphitheater, the domination of the proceedings by a big-city boss, the deep divisions in the Democratic party itself. *This*. It was a word for events and feelings that still wanted words and that had yet to achieve an authentic voice, inside or outside political conventions. *This* is the legacy of Chicago that the Democrats carry into the 1968 campaign.

Any convention—with its confusion, its uncertainty, and its brokerage-in-power—can produce paranoia. This one, under Mayor Daley's management, his cops, and his propaganda, was a psychopath's dream. Learned professors went about the hall talking about "them" like so many Birchites ferreting out a Communist plot; television reporters declared they were being followed by unidentified men; and delegates remained in a state of near rebellion against almost every aspect of the proceedings from schedule to security. Even the winners—the members of Hubert Humphrey's staff—acknowledged that the convention had exacerbated rather than resolved the fissures in the party, that the street demonstrations—and the resulting brutality by police—had not helped their man, and that the Republicans' powerful instinct for losing was more than offset by the demonstrations and the tactics of the mayor of Chicago. (The McCarthy people regarded Lyndon Johnson, of course, as the lone figure in the smoke-filled room of 1968. Nonetheless, it may be that Daley rendered Humphrey—and party unity—the greatest of services by replacing LBJ as the central figure of the convention. He made it easier for Humphrey to become his own man.

Humphrey now faces the problem of giving his liberal constituents and supporters the voice they lost in Chicago: immediately after the nomination nearly one thousand people—many of them McCarthy kids—attended an organizational meeting for Marcus Raskin's New Party. (Several hundred more, while remaining in the party, declared that —at least for the moment—they would not support the Humphrey-Muskie ticket.) Most of them were not delegates or, even in the remotest sense, politicians. They were college students, housewives, academics, and a host of other newcomers to political activism.

Nonetheless, they did represent much of what was new and exciting and hopeful on the fringe of the Democratic Party, and many of them spoke and acted as if they were never going to have anything to do with Democrats again. "The Democratic Party," said a young man who was still carrying his walkie-talkie, "is dead." It was not so much that they felt betrayed by the party bosses—by *them*—or that they despaired in defeat after nine months of hard campaigning, but that they were convinced that the party as a system, an institution, was no longer viable, no matter who controlled it. In their view, Hubert Humphrey was nominated not because the conventional processes had failed, but because they had functioned too well. "None of

those people on the National Committee is under seventy,"
said an angry Congressman from California. "The institutions have prevailed—the unions, the politicians—the god-
damn institutions."

In fact, the McCarthy campaign and the challenge to
the administration position on Vietnam came a lot further
in nine months of campaigning than anyone could have
anticipated in the days when Allard K. Lowenstein, a
young New York Democrat, first suggested that Lyndon
Johnson should, and could, be dropped from the 1968
ticket, and even further since Eugene McCarthy took his
kiddie corps into New Hampshire. The dovish Vietnam
challenge, which called for an immediate bombing halt,
lost, but not until after 40 percent of the convention delegates had voted against the administration, and not until
the convention—and the nation—had been allowed to hear
two hours of debate on the issue.

More significant for the future of the party is the abo-
lition of the unit rule, which made it possible for men such
as Governor John Connally of Texas to control large dele-
gations and deliver them en masse (in this instance) to the
Johnson Vietnam plank. No member of the so-called Texas
challenge delegation—which included a substantial number
of Negroes and Mexican-Americans, which had the support of Senator Ralph Yarborough, and which represented
some 40 percent of the Texas electorate—was seated in
Chicago. Under the new rule, which covers county and
precinct conventions as well as the state convention, that
sort of misrepresentation should be a thing of the past.
Even this year, it was Lester Maddox who went home and
Julian Bond, the young Negro legislator from Atlanta,
who stayed. Mississippi was represented by Fannie Lou
Hamer, and by a group of liberals—black and white—and
not by Senator James O. Eastland. Negroes, to be certain,

were underrepresented—though not nearly to the extent they were at the Republican convention in Miami—yet there were enough of them to hold the first black caucus to take place at any national political convention.

And yet, Hubert Humphrey and the Democrats will still have trouble speaking for hundreds of thousands, if not millions, of disaffected Americans who regard him (and Richard Nixon) as a voice of the past and as a representative of a compromising, unimaginative political style. For all his charm and power, Humphrey has become the anti-hero to many young Democrats—bland, somewhat out of date, a sort of pre-modern man. As they speak of him, he is tainted not only by service in the Johnson administration but by twenty years in public office. Perhaps he has been around too long. The excessive exposure of television may tend to shorten the public life of any public man.

More than anything, however, Humphrey still bears the stigma of Vietnam and of association with the party in power, and he therefore becomes a target for public frustration with existing policies. "The American people are deeply discontented with the direction of the country," said Richard Goodwin, who had worked for McCarthy. "The issue is whether they'll turn to people like McCarthy or to the Max Raffertys and George Wallaces." Humphrey's liability, the party's liability, is that they still stand—by and large—for a liberalism that is, at least for the moment, on the decline. Without doubt Humphrey will be, as he claims, his own man, "the captain of the team." In his acceptance speech and in subsequent statements he has already indicated that he will not be inflexibly bound by the policies of the past. There is little doubt, moreover, that in regard to Vietnam he came close to a break with President Johnson. It was only by direct intervention—through people such as John Connally and through personal emissaries in Chicago—that Johnson blocked the adoption of a compromise plank in the platform.

Yet even if Humphrey is his own man, can he be President, too? In an ironic way, Humphrey was the Eugene McCarthy of 1948, the man who took up unpopular causes and developed a reputation for political courage when his liberalism was radical, when it stood clearly to the left of the mainstream. What remains of it now seems pallid by comparison because the Humphreys have won their battles and the lonely men speak a different language. Humphrey spoke well—to the Indiana delegation, for example—of his record in reforming the city of Minneapolis, and of his civil rights battles in the Senate, but no one under thirty seemed interested. "Who cares about things that happened twenty years ago," said a young reporter who stood in the room.

If Humphrey has trouble rallying the supporters of Senator McCarthy, who has indicated that he will not support the national ticket, he may have even more difficulty in reassembling the coalition of ethnic and labor groups which have, since 1932, been the backbone of the Democratic Party. The real splits in the party, despite the rhetoric of the McCarthy forces, are not only those between liberals and bosses, or between Johnson hawks and McCarthy doves, but between lower-middle-class populism and a liberal middle-class vision that divides the nation into "slums and suburbs."

When Richard Nixon and George Wallace appeal to the "forgotten man," they are speaking to several million whites—garage mechanics, taxi drivers, stevedores, shopkeepers, cops, firemen, and trade union members—many of them former Democrats, who are caught in an inflationary financial squeeze between affluence and welfare, who have neither the amenities of wealth nor the benefits of new social programs. Until Wallace began his campaign, these were, without doubt, the most alienated and disregarded people in America. For nearly a decade they have not had a psychic home in national politics. Most social commentators and politicians saw the nation as either affluent or black; the lower-middle-class white was left out altogether, or was simply labeled a bigot when he opposed integration. The various civil rights laws, the poverty program, and the general concern about Negroes did not apply to him, excepting only those instances when suburbanites demanded that he integrate *his* schools and *his* neighborhood.

When Mayor Daley's cops beat and gassed the peace demonstrators and the hippies in Chicago, they were doing the work of the lower-middle-class white; for him, at least, Daley is not merely a boss, but a man with a constituency of working men and white ethnic groups. For every hippie in Chicago there are twenty, or perhaps a hundred, local citizens who proclaim their love for the Mayor. When Nixon and Wallace—and now Humphrey—call for law and order, they are, at least in part, appealing to them and articulating their demands. Despite the liberal protests about the Chicago police—despite Senator Abraham Ribicoff's courageous remarks about Gestapo tactics in the streets of Chicago—one of the biggest cheers at the convention went to Congressman Wayne Hays of Ohio when he attacked those who substituted "beards for brains" and when he congratulated Daley and the Chicago police. In their shouting vengeful enthusiasm, the delegates who whooped it up for Hays and Daley may have been the most violent people in town. The majority in Chicago may have been out of touch with the young, but they were in touch with the mood of America.

The mood is new and there appear to be new constituencies and groups to express it. It is not merely the

Democratic Party that is split; what is breaking apart is the great New Deal consensus that has given American politics its order since 1932. The professionals in both parties declare that when November comes most of those now supporting Wallace or McCarthy will return to one of the major parties. In the South, Nixon is campaigning with a slogan that a vote for Wallace is a wasted vote. Humphrey, reading the signs—and perhaps his own heart —has declared at least qualified support for Daley: Most Americans, despite the televised police brutality, appear to side with the Chicago police, not with the demonstrators. This is not the year, say the Humphrey people (and also the Nixon people) for new programs in social welfare, for a New Deal or a New Frontier or a Great Society. It is the year of law and order.

Perhaps most of the disaffected American voters will come back to one of the major parties, if not in November, then in 1970 or 1972, yet the signs at this moment are inconclusive. Wallace will not only capture several states in the Deep South (the Humphrey forces have already given up Alabama, Mississippi, Louisiana, and Georgia—though they still have hopes for Texas, North Carolina, and Florida), but he will also receive a visible minority of the Northern labor vote. In some unions, according to incomplete polls, he has 30 percent of the vote. Union leaders deny the accuracy of the polls, but they are undoubtedly worried. George Meany marched with Humphrey, both in Chicago and in the Labor Day parade in New York, but he may well be looking around to see who will follow in November.

Wallace will probably cost Nixon more votes than he takes from Humphrey. There are California liberals, for example, who feel that the only hope for Humphrey in that state is the damage Wallace does to Nixon among

southern California conservatives. More important, however, is what Wallace takes from both major candidates.
Even if the election does not go to the House, a large
Wallace vote will make a powerful impact on American
politics, just as Wallace's campaign has already begun to
make an impact on the major parties. To many voters,
both Nixon and Humphrey are men of an older establishment—comfortable, somewhat elitist, detached. Wallace is
clearly a candidate of the Right. But he is also a carrier
of a populist impulse that was once a segment of the New
Deal mainstream, part egalitarianism, part socialism, part
cussedness, part bigotry. If Wallace does well, he will send
both parties on a frantic courtship of his constituents. The
forgotten man (white) now has, or feels he has, a national
voice.

Humphrey, of course, has barely begun to fight. He has
always been an effective campaigner. Unlike Nixon, he
has not lost a partisan election in twenty years. His supporters in Chicago and his own staff acknowledge that he
has run behind in the polls, but those polls, they say, were
taken when no candidate was definite, when "the situation
was unsettled and explosive." The liberals, said a member
of the staff, have no quarrel with him on domestic policy;
he is, after all, a vocal advocate and supporter of Great
Society programs. On Vietnam, according to members
of his staff, Humphrey will make a clear break with the
established policy if he is not spared the problem by
events in Paris. "Now that Hanoi knows that there's no
point in waiting for the election," said a member of the
campaign staff, "the North Vietnamese may be more willing to negotiate. He may lose some of those kids, but the
kids can't vote anyway."

Nonetheless, the enthusiasm of the delegates was mixed.
"A lot of people in my delegation," said a Texan, "are

going home to vote for Nixon." Politicians such as Daley would have preferred Edward Kennedy because they are doubtful that Humphrey can win, but most will support Humphrey because he is their candidate, and party loyalty demands it. "He'll be just as strong as Nixon for law and order," said a member of the Massachusetts delegation. "I prefer Humphrey because he's a Democrat."

Once Humphrey begins to campaign—concentrating on the cities of the North, on California, and on labor—he can make it a good, tough partisan fight, running not only against Nixon but also against Spiro Agnew and Strom Thurmond. "Nixon's running against the Negroes," said a Texas liberal, a view that can be reinforced without ever saying it in public. Humphrey, given time, can get away from the embarrassment of his convention. Perhaps Humphrey's major problem will be to find an effective response to Nixon's simplistic call for law and order. Humphrey missed an opportunity—at least with the liberals in the party—when he failed to denounce the brutality of the Chicago cops, a brutality that was unwarranted under any standard of security or order. There were plans, he said, to assassinate the major candidates, and burn down the Hilton Hotel. Yet, as the leaders of the demonstration pointed out, arsonists and assassins don't do their work chanting peace slogans and singing songs in the park.

There is hardly a question that the Democratic Party will survive its wounds from Chicago—will even survive the divisions in American society, divisions between hawks and doves, between young and old, between black and white, even between those who still believe in the efficacy of established political institutions and those who do not and who have taken to the streets. (The Republicans survived Goldwater and the disaffections he produced, and they seem now to be stronger than ever.) The question is:

In what form will the Democratic party survive and with what justification?

During the week of the convention, Chicago became not only a meeting place for politicians of every stripe and persuasion, it became a microcosm of American society at large—the ugly, the commonplace, the magnificent. In the lobbies of the hotels, and in the streets outside, McCarthy kids argued with peace marchers, demonstrators with national guardsmen, black militants with white liberals. Alongside the placards and buttons of the politicians were the peace posters, broadsides proclaiming BUSTS BEGIN, signs headed THE PEOPLE VS. HUMPHREY, and chants of "Dump the Hump." Within a hundred yards of the Conrad Hilton one could hear soul music sponsored by Humphrey; see Dick Gregory and Ralph Abernathy speaking to the demonstrators in Grant Park, and listen to residents of South Chicago declaring that the demonstrators were not real American kids, that they were uncouth and unattractive.

Every one of these groups and individuals is making claims on the party; every one must either be accommodated or be relegated to the streets. What angered the liberal elements most was the fact that this theater of the absurd—demonstrations, police, delegates, hippies, convention security—was held together by Mayor Daley. Because Daley was the bridge between the convention and the streets, and because he played a major role in both, it was his political and personal style that colored the proceedings.

Still another style and other possibilities were clearly visible. The very fact that there was so much confrontation, and that several hundred delegates from every part of America saw things they had never believed possible —that they saw *this*—and that they marched in protest, indicates that other forces are being heard and felt. The line between the best and the worst in Chicago was relatively narrow. Under other circumstaces, this might have been Robert Kennedy's or even Hubert Humphrey's convention—not Daley's—and the proceedings might have been held together by optimism rather than despair or fear.

No one knows how much difference leadership and rhetoric make, yet it is clear that many of the disaffected —from Vietnam doves to Wallace populists—regarded Bobby Kennedy as the best alternative. The appeal of Robert Kennedy—and perhaps ultimately of Edward Kennedy, who was an omnipresent offstage figure—transcended rational political calculations. The appeal was on personality; surely death and hindsight augmented that appeal, yet it was there and it manifested itself in a brief boom for Edward Kennedy. Within two days several hundred delegates had signed petitions urging the young Kennedy to run, despite the fact that he has virtually no experience or record worthy of a serious Presidential candidate. Within two days scores and perhaps hundreds of young men and women appeared at the Sherman House to hand-letter posters and canvass delegates on behalf of a man who had, at that moment, only the slimmest chance of nomination.

Most of those who came to Chicago are going to remain somewhere in or around the Democratic Party, even if they don't support Humphrey with great enthusiasm. Some will work for local candidates, others will wait for someone like Edward Kennedy in 1972. The anger of people like Lowenstein, Senate candidate Paul O'Dwyer of New York, and Congressman Philip Burton of California derives not from cynicism about the party but from frustrated optimism. They have a sense that the parliamentary rigidity

of the party and its convention—and their unwillingness to
bend for a moderate Vietnam plank—were unnecessary
stupidities. They couldn't get their literature on the floor,
although the Humphrey forces did; couldn't get recognition from the chair, which deferred to Daley when the
crucial parliamentary decisions were made. Daley even
controlled the band, and ordered it to play over the protesting "We Shall Overcome" that was sung by some of
the New York delegates.

Humphrey was going to be nominated anyway, the liberals said. Through moderation and tolerance toward
views and ideas from a wide spectrum of American politics,
the party might gain at least some of the strength and
enthusiasm offered by the new people in Chicago. They
were, in short, reformers-from-within: they didn't want
to drive people into the streets, were not trying to prove
conventional politics corrupt and hopeless. They wanted
the party to extend itself, and to grow. But this was not
their year, either in Chicago or—if Chicago reflected anything at all—in America. It might have been difficult even
for a Kennedy to turn the convention around.

And yet—despite all the furor, despite the bosses, the
brawls, despite the police and Mayor Daley—America went
to Chicago, and not Miami. David Dellinger and the other
organizers of the peace demonstrations said they came
here—rather than going to Miami—because the Democrats
are the party in power and therefore have the major
responsibility for Vietnam and the war machine. Yet
clearly they also came to Chicago because, in some sense,
the Democrats are their party, because historically, and
perhaps emotionally, they belonged or once subscribed
to the Democratic position. They are not about to return
to the party or to any conventional form of politics, yet
undoubtedly they felt that they were more likely to be

heard and respected here than in Miami and that, at least, they had a better claim on this party than on the other.

Given the situation in contemporary politics, a similar phenomenon at the Republican convention would have been all but inconceivable. It is even more inconceivable— in 1968—to think of a Republican Eugene McCarthy. Vietnam is, after all, Lyndon Johnson's War. Yet it was Lyndon Johnson's party and not the Republicans that came within a respectable distance of disavowing it before the world.

The point is simply that the choice for political reform is still between the Democratic Party, a totally new and still unimagined set of institutions, and the streets. For the Democratic candidates this is both an opportunity and a frightful responsibility. Much of what happened in Chicago justified and verified what the radicals among the peace demonstrators claimed: that the Democrats could only nominate a candidate in the setting of a police state, that the existing political processes are decadent, that the police are brutal, and that new institutions (or no institutions) are in order. What Chicago did was cut some more ground from the middle; it strengthened the radicals and the repressors, weakened the moderates, and heightened the frustrations. It made the campaign even harder for Humphrey and Muskie because they are middle-ground liberals and it is that shrinking middle ground on which they must run. It will be a long and probably an ugly campaign. Wherever the politicians go, the demonstrators will be out. And there are undoubtedly places to which they can no longer go at all.

[1968]

WHY OUR SCHOOLS HAVE FAILED

In the context of traditional American belief, Section 402 of the Civil Rights Act of 1964 is one of the simplest, most unambiguous directives ever issued to a government agency. It instructs the United States Commissioner of Education to carry out a survey "concerning the lack of availability of equal educational opportunities for individuals by reason of race, color, religion, or national origin in educational institutions" in the United States and its possessions. Presumably, the wording of Section 402 merely pointed toward an examination of the effects of overt racial discrimination in American schools. What it produced instead was a 737-page document that demonstrated not only the ineffectiveness of schools in overcoming the handicaps of poverty and deprivation, but also the fact that no one knows what the phrase "equal educational opportunities" means, and that, given the conditions of contemporary American society, it can have no meaning. Education in America is patently unequal, it is structured to be unequal, and it can only define its successes by its failures. On the dark side of every conception of "opportunity" lies an equal measure of exclusion and rejection.

No one needs another set of statistics to prove that American Negro children—and many others—are being miseducated, that they are behind in the elementary grades, and that they fall further behind as they move through school. In the twelfth grade, more than 85 percent of Negro children score below the average white on standardized tests of achievement, their dropout rates are higher, and their self-esteem is lower. We can dispute the validity of the tests as indicators of intelligence, but there is not the slightest doubt that if they measure educational achievement, and if they predict future success in school and college (as they do), then the children of the poor minorities in America perform well below average. What the new statistics do provide is solid evidence for the repeated assertion by civil-rights leaders and others that what children learn in school are the rules and attitudes of second-class citizenship, and that the school is a highly effective mechanism not only for advancement but for selecting people out.

Historically, "equality of educational opportunity" simply demanded that all individuals were to have access to similar resources in similar public schools: where children failed, it was because of their own limitations, their

lack of ambition and intelligence, not because of the inadequacies of the schools or the society. If the schools
were found to favor a particular race or economic group
(as they were in many of the desegregation cases), one
could rectify the inequities through application of
relatively simple standards: the appropriation of equal resources to the education of children of all races, the integration of schools, or the reassignment of teachers. The
definition never contemplated the difficulties children
might bring from home or the fact that even the best
teachers and resources, according to the conventional
standards, were keyed to middle-class experience, motivation, and attitude. More important, it never contemplated
genuine integration: what it presumed was that only the
white middle-class society offered ideals and standards
of value, and that whatever the ghetto offered, or what
minority children brought with them, was to be disregarded, deflated, or denied. The traditional melting pot
was stirred by Protestant hands with a white ladle.

It will be years before the sociologists and statisticians
get through with the data in the government's report,
Equality of Educational Opportunity, that was prompted
by Section 402. The study, headed by Professor James S.
Coleman of the Johns Hopkins University, was eighteen
months in the making, cost $2 million to produce, and
included data on six hundred thousand children and sixty
thousand teachers in four thousand schools. It is written,
as Christopher Jencks said, "in the workmanlike prose of
an Agriculture Department bulletin on fertilizer," and it
is so thoroughly crammed with tables, regression coefficients, and standard deviations as to make all but the
most passionate statisticians shudder. (Ultimately, as it
turned out, even some of the statisticians began to shudder.) Nonetheless, the Coleman Report has probably be-

come the most influential educational study of the decade. It formed the basis of the recent report of the United States Civil Rights Commission, *Racial Isolation in the Public Schools*, it provided ammunition for a federal court opinion on segregation in the Washington schools, it is the topic of conferences and seminars, it is endlessly quoted at meetings, and it became the subject of a year-long study at Harvard under the direction of Daniel P. Moynihan and Thomas Pettigrew (who also wrote the Civil Rights Commission Report). It may be a measure of the times that, where forty years ago we produced educational philosophy and ideology, we are now producing statistics.

The Coleman Report comes to two central conclusions:

(1) That the most significant determinant of educational success (as measured by standardized tests of mathematical and verbal performance) is the social and economic background of the individual student, that formal instructional inputs—which are not as unequally distributed between races as supposed—make relatively little difference, and that the social and economic composition of fellow students, not materials or libraries, is the most important in-school resource.

(2) That children from disadvantaged backgrounds (regardless of race) benefit from integration with advantaged kids (regardless of race), but that the latter are not harmed by such integration. Proper integration mixes rich and poor and produces a general social gain: the poor learn more; the performance of the rich does not go down.

The Coleman conclusions substantiate propositions that have been gaining currency in the last few years. If racial integration is pedagogically desirable, then clearly social and economic integration, and the interplay of cultural styles, are even more important. Poor blacks and whites can learn from each other, but rich and poor—under the proper conditions—can benefit even more. The report's conclusions on the impact of teachers are not entirely clear, but they do indicate that good teachers and effective educational environments are more important to the disadvantaged than to those who have access (in the home, for example) to other resources. Even so, teachers, libraries, laboratories, and other formal inputs are not as important as fellow students.

Carried to its ultimate, the Coleman Report seems to indicate that schools make relatively little difference, except as a place where kids learn from each other, and that money spent in improving them is likely, at best, to yield marginal results. The first temptation, of course, is to dismiss that assertion as an absurdity: we take it as an article of faith that the public school has always been the great American social instrument, the device that converted the raw material of immigration into an endless stream of social success. Now, oddly enough, the school seems to be failing in the very functions on which its reputation has always been based. It does not seem to be able to bring the most indigenous and American of all "immigrants" into the mainstream or even to give them the educational qualifications that life in the mainstream requires. Given the insights of recent experience, we might now properly ask whether the school was ever as successful or important in the process of Americanization and education as the history textbooks sentimentally picture it. With the possible exception of the Jews, did the school ever become a major avenue of entry for the ethnic minorities of the urban centers? How effective was it for the Irish, the Italians, the Poles? Was it the school or the street that acculturated our immigrants? What about such Americanizing institutions as the political ward, the shop, and the small town? A half-century ago American society provided alternatives to formal education, and no one became officially distressed about dropouts and slow readers. Now the school has become *the* gatekeeper to advancement, and while it is being blamed for obvious failures, it may actually be doing better than it ever did before.

And yet, despite the accumulation of studies and statistics, we still don't know how much difference formal education makes, except to amplify characteristics that have already been determined somewhere else. The Coleman *conclusions* indicate that it doesn't make much difference, but here semantic problems and statistical difficulties begin to get in the way. What the Coleman group did was, in essence, to take schools with students of similar background and try to determine how much difference varying inputs seemed to make. (For example, given two all-Negro schools, did children in the school where teachers had better training and higher degrees perform better than those in the other school?) In controlling for student background, however, Coleman and his colleagues may have underestimated the crucial fact that almost all schools are internally harmonious systems, and that where children come from disadvantaged backgrounds their teachers are also likely, in some respects, to be disadvantaged. Two economists, Samuel Bowles of Harvard and Henry M. Levin of the Brookings Institution, point out in the *Journal of Human Resources* that if the methodology of the study had been reversed, so would the conclusions: that is, if Coleman had controlled for such educational inputs as teacher training, the social background of the students would have appeared to make little difference. They point out, moreover, that the Coleman Report, despite the vast sample, was unavoidably biased through the refusal of many school systems to furnish data: suburban systems were statistically over-represented while big cities, which have the most severe problems, were under-represented. The most vicious attribute of urban school systems, until recently, has not been their consistent failure with the disadvantaged, but their refusal to produce honest data on that failure. In case after case, they pretended (perhaps because of the historical definition of "equality") that despite statistical evidence to the contrary it was individual children, not schools, that failed. Bowles and Levin contend, moreover, that the Coleman Report's conclusions that teachers' traits (verbal facility, educational level, etc.) are relatively unimportant are not supported by the data, which suggest exactly the opposite; that the report's data on the importance of class size are useless, and that its conclusions about the effect of integration are questionable since "the processes of residential and academic selection imply that those Negroes who attend predominantly white schools are drawn largely from higher social strata." In brief, integration is educationally effective among those who are already educationally and socially "advantaged."

The most significant difficulty, however, is one that the Coleman Report did not create and cannot solve. What does equality mean in education? Does it mean that the average Negro should be doing as well as the average white, and that the resources devoted to his education should be improved until he does? Or does it point to some sort of parity in resources? Or to something else? Coleman himself said that the focus of his report was not on "what resources go into education, but on what product comes out." He then goes on to say (in an article in *The Public Interest*) that "equality of educational opportunity implies not merely 'equal' schools but equally effective schools, whose influences will overcome the differences in starting point of children from different social groups."

Pedagogically and politically, Coleman's suggestion is pleasant, impossible, and probably undesirable. Pleasant because it has a nice democratic ring, impossible because the haves in the society won't allow it to happen, undesirable because it assumes that all social and cultural differences should be equalized away, that Negro children (or Chinese or Jews) have nothing to offer *as Negroes* except problems and disadvantage, and that their culture (or perhaps even their genes) gives them nothing special that might be socially, educationally or personally valuable. A Negro in this context is nothing but a disadvantaged white.

Since we are now beginning to discover the crucial importance of the very early years of childhood, it is likely that we can achieve a greater measure of equality—to narrow the gap between the advantaged and disadvantaged. More effective preschool programs, and a general extension of the social responsibility of the school for children from deprived homes, may make the classroom more effective. But the matter of achieving genuine equality is another question.

As to the politics: the most effective way that a middle-class parent can endow his children is by buying them a superior education, by giving them the head start his advantages can provide, and he is not likely to run slower to let the poor catch up. Given Coleman's standards, the only way to determine whether schools "overcome the differences in starting point of children from different social groups" is when Negro children from Harlem do as well in College Board scores or reading achievement as whites from Scarsdale. Yet when that happens, Scarsdale will have lost its reason to exist. Is the average white afraid of integration or "equality" only because the Negroes would, as he often says, "drag down the standards" or also because, ultimately, they might succeed? What would happen if the prep schools and suburban high schools, let alone the Ivy League universities, were no longer a guarantee of advantage and ultimate success? What if the game were genuinely open? It has often been said that American economic viability depended in part on the existence of a class of individuals who were available for the dirty jobs that the society requires (try the suggestion that we guarantee everyone a living wage, and listen to the prophecies of economic doom), but is it not equally conceivable that, for many, self-esteem and success are themselves defined by the failures of others? We can assert that technology is taking us to some sort of economic nirvana in which menial work is superfluous and we will no longer require Negroes to do it. And yet, doesn't the psychology of success always require a class of failures, and aren't the black, by virtue of their cultural inheritance, always the best candidates? Can we ever maintain a middle class without a lower class, or does it thrive, like Alcoholics Anonymous, on the continued presence of a group of people who, it is assumed, need reform, and from whose failures the successful can draw esteem? Even if we dismiss that as the bleakest kind of cynicism, we are still confronted by the difficulty of a system where cash and power are convertible into educational assets, where educational assets are, in turn, the major qualifications for entry into the life and prerogatives of the middle class, and where the poor have neither. No governmental program is likely to alleviate the inequities.

As to the pedagogy: Coleman's assumption in talking about the different starting points of children "from different social groups" is that all talent is equally distributed through the population, and that inequities are generated only by social rather than ethnic or cultural characteristics. The current evidence seems to make the assumption doubtful: it points, indeed, to a very different course of action from the one Coleman advocates. For years there was a lot of condescending talk about the attributes and activities of different ethnic groups (all Jews were tailors, the Chinese ran laundries, the Negro had "rhythm"), and we properly reacted with egalitarian indignity when we decided how silly and pernicious that talk had become. Are we now going overboard the other way by suggesting that all talents and interests, of whatever kind, are distributed absolutely equally through the different ethnic sectors of the population? In establishing criteria for academic success—indeed for social success generally—are we emphasizing certain skills and measures at the expense of others that may be equally valuable not only to the individual's personality and self-esteem but to the society generally? In a recent article in the *Harvard Educational Review*, Susan S. Stodolsky and Gerald Lesser report on research that indicates that the relative strengths and weaknesses in different attributes remain constant for various ethnic groups, regardless of whether they are middle- or lower-class. Jews, for example, score higher, relative to the general population, in verbal ability than they do in space conceptualization. For Chinese children, the relative strengths and weaknesses in verbal ability and space conceptualization are reversed. (Similarly, Negroes seem to perform somewhat better in arithmetic skills and space conceptualization than they do in verbal tests; for Puerto Ricans, the pattern is almost the reverse.) Although middle-class children score higher in *all categories*, the relative ethnic differences are not eliminated. To Lesser and Stodolsky, these findings suggest new distinctions, definitions, and a new course of action. To Coleman's call for equalization, they want to add what they consider the equally important objective of diversification, of trading on the strengths of different ethnic groups, and helping them to develop those strengths to the maximum. "Beyond deploying all necessary resources to achieve minimal equality in essential goals, further development of students may well be diverse," they write. "Following our principle of matching instruction and ability we incidentally may enhance the initial strengths which each group possesses. For example, through the incidental enhancement of the space-conceptualization skills of the Chinese children, we may produce proportionally more Chinese than Jewish architects and engineers. Conversely, through incidental enhancement of verbal skills of the Jewish children, we may produce proportionally more Jewish than Chinese authors or lawyers." There is no suggestion here about producing a Jewish or a Chinese curriculum; what they do propose is tailoring the mode and techniques of instruction to the strengths of particular children.

Studies like this are a long way from producing comprehensive solutions, but they demonstrate how complex the problem has become, how little we know about learning, and how ineffective most current remedial programs seem to be. One of the difficulties, indeed, is determining just what the problem really is. The Coleman Report, whatever its weaknesses, has made the definitional problem painfully clear. When we talk about the education of Negroes, or urban schools, or the ghetto, are we talking about ethnic minorities, a social class, or simply the universal difficulties of operating effective schools, no matter who their pupils happen to be? Clearly there is validity in the charge that some teachers are racially and socially biased, and that the phrase "cultural disadvantage" can be used, like assertions about Negro inferiority, as an excuse for failure, a cop-out for bad teachers. The psychologist Kenneth B. Clark has often pointed out that statements about uneducable children tend to become self-fulfilling prophecies, and that teachers who talk this way don't belong in the classroom. At the same time, it's hard to believe that the same attitudes don't operate in classrooms full of lower-class Italians or Appalachian mountaineers, or that the Protestant schoolmarms of the year 1900 were altogether openminded about the Jews and the Catholics.

Before anyone comes back with the declaration that "we made it on our own, why can't they?" let's quickly add that the economy that permitted making "it" on one's own is dead and gone, and that when it comes to many contemporary school systems, *all children* tend to be disadvantaged. What I'm suggesting is that many schools are not educational but sociological devices which destroy learning and curiosity and deny differences as often as they encourage them, and which value managerial order above initiative, good behavior above originality, and mediocrity above engagement. (Yes, of course, there are exceptions.) All too often, they demand styles of behavior antithetical not only to social and ethnic minorities, but also to most other original or "difficult" children, no matter what their background. They are instruments of social selection, and as such they screen out misfits for the middle class, regardless of race, color, or national origin. In performing this function, every guidance counselor becomes an immigration officer and every examination a petition for a passport. The school, in short, is not an instrument of pluralism, but of conformity. It turns out shoddy goods for the dime-store trade; its teachers are not professionals but petty civil servants who teach children to deny their own instincts and honesty, teach them little tricks of evasion, and reject those who are not acceptable for the mold. While the deviants of the upper class may have access to special schools in the suburbs or the hills of New England, the poor have no choice: the law *requires* them to go to one particular school in one community which, as often as not, treats them as inmates. The school in this instance becomes a sort of colonial outpost manned by a collection of sahibs from downtown. Their idea of community relations is telling parents to encourage their kids to stay in school, help them with their homework, and live the life of Dick and Jane. As a result, the neighborhood school is in, but not of or by the neighborhood.

Given these conditions and the failures of the ghetto schools, the current demands for decentralization and community control are hardly surprising. There is nothing radical about them, except in the view of school personnel who have been trained to suspect community pressure and who regard any overt mixture of politics and education as the ultimate evil. The advocates of decentralization, who feel that ghetto parents should have as much control over the education of their children as the parents of the small suburb, see political action as the only way to make the school effective and responsible: the issue is not a black principal or a black curriculum for their own sake, but making the schools accountable, and developing the sense of participation that is expected to come with it. If parents are involved, they may provide the interest and support that the education of their children requires. The schools will then become *their* schools, the teachers *their* teachers. A principal working for parents is going to try harder than one who is responsible only to bureaucrats downtown.

For many militants, the appeal of decentralization—as an essential component of community power (read Black Power, if preferred)—is extremely powerful. At the same time, the concept of decentralization suffers from some serious ambiguities. There are people like Roy Innis, a leader in CORE, who favor a single Negro school district in Harlem, a system as distinct from that of New York City as the schools of Buffalo. For most others, including white liberals, the model is a collection of small districts, each hopefully resembling those of the suburbs or the small town, each immediately accessible to the parents and community. The difference between the two is as large as the difference between Thomas Jefferson and John C. Calhoun: one visualizes a thoroughgoing decentralization—educational federalism; the other calls forth the ghost of the doctrine of the concurrent majority. It is based on the presumption that the Negro community is as distinct from the mainstream as the peculiar institution which helped give it birth and on which Calhoun founded his brand of separatism more than a century ago. Both suffer from what may be an excessive belief in the power of formal education and a conviction that racism and bad intentions, rather than educational incompetence, are the major sources of educational inadequacy.

Yet if this were the whole problem—if teachers and schools were guilty of nothing more than middle-class bias or political irresponsibility toward the poor—the situation would not be as difficult as it is. Even if one grants the possibility of effective decentralization as a *political* solution (assuming that parents can run schools without turning them into political battlegrounds or hothouses of nepotism), what of the educational solutions? The pressure for decentralization does not stem from some specific educational program that large systems refuse to adopt and which the militants consider appropriate to the problems of their neighborhoods and children. Indeed, if the Coleman Report has any validity—and there is little reason to doubt that children from different social backgrounds do learn from each other—then decentralization, which will help institutionalize segregation, is a step backward. Thus, the Bundy Report, which outlines a plan of decentralization for New York City, and the Coleman Report, one might think, were composed on different planets.

The great possibility of decentralization (in New York, the proposal is to establish between thirty and sixty semi-autonomous districts) is not some large educational breakthrough, but no more, and no less, than the immediate objective itself: giving the community a greater sense of participation and voice in the management of one of its institutions. (In this respect, it is no different from increasing community control over planning, street cleaning, or the administration of the local precinct of the police.) It is thus a revolt against the "professionals"— the people who took charge, in the name of reform and good government, and apparently failed to deliver the goods. In its unwillingness to trust the experts, the demand for decentralization is frontier populism come to the city, a rejection of outside planning and expertise. Parents whose children attend decentralized schools may (with luck) learn more about political action and school management than their children learn about reading or mathematics; so far, at any rate, the chances for the first outweigh those of the second. The mystery of power is, for the moment, more fascinating than the problems of instruction.

The fact is that no one, in the ghetto or out, has yet developed a vision of what the ghetto schools ought to do, how they should operate, or what an educated Negro child ought to be if he is to be something different from a dark-skinned middle-class white. The existing ghetto schools fail Negroes not so much because they are different from all other schools—as the integrationists once assumed—but because they are too much like them. Local control may introduce diversity and new ideas, but those changes are far from clear. At this point there are few alternative models to the existing public-school program. The current talk about relevance in Negro education—about more Afro-Americanism in the curriculum, about Negro history, about urban problems—and the peripheral efforts to use the arts (painting, the dance, music) as ways of engaging children's interests have not taken us very far toward genuine educational integration, toward the point, that is, where ghetto children have the skills to compete effectively in the larger world. It has been said again and again that conventional instruction in formalized academic skills is difficult for children whose lives provide few examples of the value of formal education and little reinforcement for work that might pay off in some vague abstract future. Middle-class kids are, in some measure, to the manner born, and they find plenty of reinforcement around them: they often succeed regardless of school. For many ghetto children, instruction, to be successful, has to be immediately attractive or interesting. (There are, to be sure, many ghetto children from families whose ambitions are identical with those of the middle class.) Whether or not "enjoyment," as someone said, "is a prerequisite to competence," it is plain that skills for the larger world may appear only remotely valuable in the immediate life of a child. The humanity of children may be very distant from the problems of negotiating the economy. The problem is how to get from one to the other.

The proposals for solving the problem are endless and, as might be expected, they are often contradictory. There is no consistent Negro demand in education, any more than there is a white one. Some Negro parents are as committed to authoritarian teachers and rote learning as the village schoolmarm; others regard them as racially repressive and pedagogically useless. (Most Negro parents are probably as conservative about education as any others.) I suspect that part of the anger and frustration in all racial school disputes stems from the inability of the parties to be entirely clear about what they want. Should the schools be more middle-class, more white than white, turning out suburban doctors and lawyers, or should they be training men and women who can cope with the outside world but whose energies are directed to the black community and whose loyalities remain in the ghetto? (The controversy is similar to a conventional school debate between advocates of vocational training and college preparation, but the race aspect charges it with explosive overtones.) Whatever the position, the issue is clear: almost inevitably it revolves around the problem of moving the child from where he is to the larger world—resolving the inconsistencies between the attitudes and experience of poverty and the formalized skills and motivation that the world demands. There is no disagreement anywhere that there is a common culture that demands certain levels of verbal and social ability. The question slowly emerging from the current debates, however, is whether that ability must become a universal virtue. Should we be concerned only with the preparation of economic functionaries and the development of conventional academic skills, or also with the growth of human beings whose dignity is not necessarily dependent on middle-class standards of success? Is an understanding of algebraic functions any more desirable than the ability to paint or dance? (The mandated requirements for many jobs—nursing, for example—include verbal abilities that are higher than those the job actually requires; the stipulated credentials are not necessarily related to the characteristics the jobs demand.) Are we establishing norms that tend to undervalue characteristics that all of society could well use, and for which certain children might be especially well prepared, or do we have to make *all* children into replicas of the middle class?

For the next several years we are likely to hear more and more along this line. In its most extreme form, the argument says that not only is the American school an instrument of the white middle class, but that the overriding emphasis—in school and out—on high verbal and cognitive skills is itself a form of racial and social bias. The rational mind, with its emphasis on a high degree of verbal and analytical facility is, in a manner of speaking, our thing. We invented and perfected it, and for the last fifteen years most curricular reform has been directed to the task of putting a larger and more powerful dose of it into the classroom. Thus we have, even more thoroughly than before, arranged education to separate the sheep of privilege from the goats of deprivation. Increasingly, we will now have to confront questions about what has been excluded: Are we missing something more intuitive, personal, and intangible? Is it possible to extend the Lesser-Stodolsky kind of analysis to include—along with assessments of verbal and mathematical characteristics, and the ability to conceptualize space—things like affective and intuitive qualities, creativity, and some general feeling for the poetic, the visual, the musical?

Because these things are difficult to test, and because their cash value has usually been remote, the schools tend to disregard them, or to assign them to a secondary level of importance. Of all the things that make life rich—the arts, the various elements of literary and personal sensitivity, social and political involvement, philosophy, religion—very few have even a minimal place (except as lip service) in the public school program. One may not be able to mandate such activities in a large compulsory school system, but it is possible to offer them as alternatives to the public school, and one can conceive of all sorts of programs for doing so. The issue here is not to turn every ghetto school into an academy of the arts, but to offer diversity—teaching the skills of a trade or an art with as much of a sense of importance as we teach mathematics or history. The objective, in each instance, is to draw upon the experiences and interests of the kids, to give them a sense of motion and relevance, and to provide choices, not only as to school and school control, but also as to style of learning. We have, with the single public system, and the instruction it offers, created a single standard of success and failure which is not acceptable even to some of those who might meet it. Perhaps we have to recognize the principle of pluralism not only in a cultural context but in an educational one as well. A few years ago such suggestions would have been regarded as racist slurs, but it is now the black militant who regards Swahili as desirable for Negroes as Latin.

Carried to its extreme, the argument leads to a romantic trap, a wishful attempt to arm the weakest members of a technological society with the least effective weapons for dealing with it. It may be nice to think that there are dishwashers with the souls of poets (or even with the skills of poets), but that thought provides no foundation on which to base an educational system. There are, in our culture, a variety of important and rewarding functions that require no extensive verbal or mathematical skills (despite the exclusionist tendency of certain trades and professions to impose arbitrary educational standards for membership). Nonetheless, there remain certain levels of verbal ability without which few people can survive, except in the most menial situations. In our ambiguity and guilt about middle-class life, many of us hold a corresponding ambiguity about those who are left outside the mainstream: the happy hillbilly, the engagement and passion of the ghetto, the uninhibited poor. What we disregard is that, given the choice, most of them would elect to live like us; because of educational deficiencies, they do not have the choice. There is, said a Negro sociologist, only one way out of the ghetto, "and that's out." The reason, finally, that so few of them make it has little to do with differences in culture, or the fact that teachers and administrators are ignorant about the lives of the children assigned to them; it is because they still don't know how to teach. Negro schools are bad because all schools are bad. We simply don't know very much about how children learn. This is, in the end, what the Coleman Report proved. It may also be the greatest single contribution of the civil rights movement.

But to say that greater diversity, the provision of educational options, and a new emphasis on intuitive learning can be carried to extremes is not to deny the validity of the idea, either in the ghetto or anywhere else. For the past decade we masculinized the schools with mathematics, physics, and with a variety of new tough-minded curricula. Educational criticism in the next decade may well concern itself more with the soft side of things—with noncognitive approaches, and with a reaffirmation of

Deweyan ideas. There are a number of people who are talking seriously about a "curriculum of concern," educational programs that begin with the interests and experience of kids, not with predetermined sets of skills to be learned. Most of the ghetto experiments that seem to have potential are pure Dewey: letting children talk their own stories and developing vocabulary and writing skills from them; trips to factories, galleries, and museums; stories and poems about the streets of the city, and even about addicts and junkies. These things, too, can be carried to undisciplined extremes. None is a cure-all, but nothing in education ever is. The very nature of the enterprise is unsettling and troublesome. Education and maturation mean change, and that, in turn, means dealing with new problems, new elements every day. Equality is relatively easy to define in employment, in housing, or in medicine. It is impossible to define in education because the very nature of the enterprise demands distinctions and produces diversity.

Are we then to abandon integration and concentrate exclusively on the problems of the classroom? Plainly the answer is no. No, because it still seems—at least to some of us—morally important; no, because, lacking better tools, it still appears to be an effective technique for education; no, because any alternative to integration is, despite immediate attractions to the contrary, unthinkable. Yet if integration is to have any meaning, it must be a two-way street—integration not only *between* races, going both ways, but also between the school and the community, school and job, culture and culture. If equality of educational opportunity means merely an effort to improve the chances of the disadvantaged to run the race on our terms, things will never be equal and whatever they have to offer will be lost. Are we really courageous enough to provide a broad range of educational options and not to worry about who's at what level in which track? Are we really interested in education or merely in grades, credits, and diplomas? In the structure of the existing school system, segregation, repression, competition, and failure are all essential parts. Every class has a bottom half, and it tends to include, numerically, as many whites as blacks. Until we are ready to stop selecting people out, almost any conception of education is going to involve some sort of segregation. Our democratic professions might be vindicated if the ranks of the successful were as well integrated as the ranks of the failures, but would that solve the problem of education? What would we do with the failures if they were a statistically average shade of tan? The fundamental issue is not the equality of Negro schools, but the lives of all young men and women, no matter what their category of stigma. "If urban educators are failing," says Robert Dentler, the director of the Center for Urban Education, "they are failing where the newly emergent culture of the urban society itself has failed to specify either ends or means for the educator or his clientele. . . . We are in a period when the place of all children in this culture is in transition." What the problem of Negro education has done, or should be doing, is to alert us to a far larger range of social and educational questions, and to the fact that the goal of maximizing human potential is still a long way off.

[1968]

THE SECRET ROOTS
OF BLACK CULTURE

The rush is on. Come and get it: Afro-Americanism, Black Studies, the Negro heritage. From Harvard to Ocean Hill, from Berkeley to Madison Avenue, they are trying, as they say, to restore the Negro to his rightful place in American history and culture—black (and white) intellectuals, scholars, teachers, politicians, hustlers busy with black restoration. The spirit is upon them, the writers and publishers, the polemicists and pushers, and the implications are enormous. But the richest soil is education, the schools and colleges, and the processes of growing up in which they're involved.

The academy is an obvious mark because it is an accessible purveyor of culture, because it tends to be guilt-ridden anyway, and because it has apparently failed black children not only in its practice but in its mythology. The school was supposed to offer—had claimed it could offer—equality, democracy, and opportunity. Instead what it provided was selectivity; it selected people in, and selected them out. By and large, black people were selected out, not because the school was independently discriminatory, but because it offered and gave what the society asked. When finally we looked inside the little black box —the mystique of education and advancement, the mystique of academic standards and professionalism—it turned out to be empty. If teachers and schools knew anything about teaching anybody (which is an open question) they plainly knew little about teaching people who did not already belong to the middle class or who refused to conform to its culture.

Black restoration was not invented inside the schools, but the intellectuals have taken it up, the students are promoting it, and the academies are debating it. Moreover, it is—for better or worse—accessible to every amateur. The line between history and mythology is indefinite, but where the first is at least theoretically subject to disciplinary standards, the latter is not. Any number can play.

Black Studies can have just as much legitimacy as anything else; if Harvard has a program on East Asia or Latin America, why not Africa? If American Negro experience has been left out of American history courses—as it has—then surely it should be restored. But the significance of black restoration—even aside from its separatist extremities (the establishment of an independent black state in America, for example)—has greater and more ambiguous implications. Is the American Negro, by whatever name, an American or an African, the heir of a separate culture, or the most indigenous of citizens? Is fiction or music produced by American Negroes uniquely a product of black experience or of an "African heritage," or is it, like all art, dependent on styles and materials from every conceivable source and tradition? Is there white art and black art in America, or just art? Is the Negro experience on this continent more significant for its uniqueness or for its human universality? "I am proud to be black," writes the sixth-grade kid in Harlem. "Say it loud: 'I am proud.'" Here it is, a response to a pile of clichés and labels, a response that may mean something, or that may be just another cliché, this one more vicious because it promised more.

For three hundred years one of the black man's problems in America has been growing up—to be a man but not a white man, to be a woman but not a chattel, to be black and visible as a complete human being. The hackneyed descriptions of self-hate and childishness may be partly the fantasy of intellectuals who are shocked that Negroes don't behave like college professors, yet clearly the price of admission to the white world has been self-denial and the willingness to play one of the stock parts by which the white world justified its own discrimination. Little Black Sambo, Uncle Tom, Uppity Nigger, House Nigger, Bourgeois Black, the urban poor. And in school, the culturally deprived, the disruptive child, "black but *bright*." Clearly all Americans have had similar problems— to grow up, to establish an adult identity on one's own terms. But it is, nonetheless, a special problem for anyone born black, and it has, in recent years, been magnified— even glorified—by the growing consciousness of the subtleties of polite discrimination.

"Each generation," wrote the Negro psychiatrists William H. Grier and Price M. Cobbs, "grows up alone." The past, it is said, exists, but it has been erased from memory, devalued, lost, and denied—denied often by the most well-meaning and liberal of Americans. Is a black man anything but a white man incomplete? Other ethnic groups seem to have the armament of a unique history and tradition—or simply the tradition of the "West"—to carry them into the mainstream. In a sense the Negro has always been in that mainstream—as a slave and servant who knew the master better than the master knew himself—but always as a Negro who could never quite aspire to full citizenship as a valid social protagonist. He was often the carrier of the culture, or even its creator: in music, in patterns of speech, in the cadences of a whole region that resented his blood but talked more of his language than it ever cared to admit. Here was the waiter who determined the appropriate status of the guests and placed them at tables according to *his* assessment of *their* merits; here was the maid who knew the secrets of the household, its triumphs and scandals; there the musician who gave art and style to generations of white performers but never, until recently, shared in the recognition. Here was a whole race that had walked through all the rooms of the white culture but had never been allowed through the front door. The problem for the Negro was that his culture and his life became too much mainstream, that it was hard to distinguish what he had done and what he had absorbed, but that it was always easy to distinguish *him* by the color of his skin.

James Baldwin once referred to himself as a "bastard of the West." There was no full citizenship—and no recognized tradition—for the black man in America, yet there was no other place to go either.

When I followed the line of my past [Baldwin wrote] I did not find myself in Europe but in Africa. And this meant that in some subtle way, in a really profound way, I brought to Shakespeare, Bach, Rembrandt, to the stones of Paris, to the cathedral of Chartres, and to the Empire State Building, a special attitude. These were not really my creations, they did not contain my history; I might search in them in vain forever for any reflection of myself. I was an interloper; this was not my heritage. At the same time I had no other heritage which I could possibly hope to use—I had certainly been unfitted for the jungle or the tribe. I would have to appropriate these white centuries. I would have to make them mine—I would have to accept my special attitude, my special place in this scheme— otherwise I would have no place in any scheme. . . .

Baldwin's problem was, and still is, the problem of every black person in America—and certainly of every black child in school. Was there a way to succeed in America without denying one's own blackness, to make it *regardless* of (not in spite of) one's Negritude? Was there a black identity beyond the limited roles that the official world allowed? One could always hustle the world, could con it, or adopt some form of Tomism, but was there a way of really making it without pretending that one was white?

Almost every black writer in America has been pre-occupied with this question, yet until recently it remained in the realm of literature. It was something that came from the imagination, and therefore wasn't quite real. Perhaps such a problem doesn't in fact exist until someone can invent a language—an imaginative form—to describe it. In this sense, then, it always remains a literary prob-lem, and the response, whether it is a child's poem or a professional's novel, is a rhetorical response. Nonetheless, the literature, and the vast amount of derivative material coming from the mimeograph machines, are expressing a new set of attitudes, giving shape to a new style of personal and political behavior, and shaping the content and practices of education. There are reasons for what that child in Harlem wrote, for the fact that there are public schools teaching Swahili, and that Malcolm X is an appropriate figure for public school commemoration.

In the past decade, perception of the Negro problem has moved in two directions: on the one hand, it has become pop sociology; on the other, it has been incorporated into a new mythology. The first is the rhetoric of the matriarchal family, the lack of father figures, the passion for a "relevant curriculum"; the second, the growth of a world of African culture, black pride, and Black Power. Preston Wilcox, who has been an intellectual spokesman for the black school movement (and is now chairman of the Association of Afro-American Educators), recently declared:

> The surge to restore the Black community in intellectual, psychological, physical, social, economic, and political terms is taking place in the form of a cultural revolution at the doorstep of the traditional Little Red Schoolhouse from which Black Americans have been planfully excluded. This culturally radical effort forces one to view the Black Restoration Movement as a nation-building activity —a process designed to build into the instinct and habit systems of Black people a need to view the many pieces of the struggle as a single conceptual response to white America's design to turn Black people away from their African heritage and their historic charge to *figuratively* return to Africa to join in the liberation struggle of Black people around the world.

Examine the language: Black Restoration, nation-building activity, the figurative return to Africa. With the exception of Marcus Garvey and his African nationalists, no American has ever talked this way before. Black Americans are not to invent an identity, or to regard themselves as complete Americans and fight for a place within the prevailing culture, they are to restore, to return, to reclaim the things that America has taken away.

The compelling central figure in this drama is not the bourgeois manager negotiating with the Establishment for more jobs or for a civil rights law, nor even a Christian martyr, but a street fighter, a hustler, a high-style liver who masters the adversities on his own terms, the man who synthesizes new meaning from familiar experience. Martin Luther King still wins the polls as "a great Negro leader," but it is the gut fighters who command the imagination. King was the ultimate Southern preacher, the man who used traditional materials—the cadences of the prayer meeting, the imperatives of the Christian witness, the moral confrontation—and improvised a new style. Suffering promised salvation even to the oppressor. His style was Baptist, Southern, and rural. The new figures are urban. They begin as compromised individuals, men who have not simply been victimized as Negroes, but who have, often joyously, participated in the underworld of the ghetto. Men like Eldridge Cleaver, Claude Brown, and Malcolm X may never become mythic heroes, but their experiences on the city streets, however untypical, are now closer to home than those of the Southern plantation. (For certain intellectuals, black and white, they may also be a way of identifying with—and romanticizing—the poor.)

The prophetic hero is Malcolm X, the man who solved the riddle of blackness, and—apparently—grew up. Other Americans had come from the depths of the common black experience, had been corrupted by the white culture, and had risen above it. Malcolm did not invent the new cosmology—Black Power, black is beautiful, think black— or the mystique of Africanism. As he tells it in the *Autobiography*, it was all revealed to him, first in prison, and later on a visit to Mecca. But it was Malcolm who delivered it to the world, who spread the gospel:

> "You don't even know who you are," Reginald [his brother] had said. "You don't even know, the white devil has hidden it from you, that you are a race of people of ancient civilizations, and riches in gold and kings. You don't even know your true family name, you wouldn't recognize your true language if you heard it. You have been cut off by the devil white man from all true knowledge of your own kind. You have been a victim of the evil of the devil white man ever since he murdered and raped and stole from your native land in the seeds of your forefathers. . . ."

All these revelations amounted to a religious experience, a transformation that he likened to the experience of St. Paul hearing the voice of Christ on the road to Damascus. What Malcolm heard was a coherent legend—a myth of plunder and conspiracy—that matched any classic tale of creation. The story came from Elijah Muhammed, the patriarch of the Muslims, whose servant Malcolm later became. According to the story, which runs for three pages in Malcolm's *Autobiography*, the first humans were black, among them the tribe of Shabazz from "which America's Negroes, so-called, descend." Among them was born a mad scientist named Mr. Yacub who was exiled with his followers. In his hatred toward Allah, Mr. Yacub created a white devil race which enslaved black men and turned what "had been a peaceful heaven on earth into a hell by quarreling and fighting." The story prophesied that this race would rule the earth for six thousand years and would then destroy itself. At that time the nonwhite people would rise again. That time was now at hand.

Malcolm eventually broke with Muhammed, and he repudiated the devil theory, but the story symbolizes the sense of racial theft that enrages the black teachers and intellectuals who are articulating the objectives of black schools and black culture. If Ben Franklin and Horatio Alger symbolized the mythology of the traditional American school—the school of hard work crowned by worldly success—Malcolm is coming to share with them a rhetorical and symbolic role in the ghetto school run by blacks. The significance of the mythology is not in its blackness, and certainly not in its disdain for hard work—Malcolm was as much of a Puritan as any Yankee schoolmarm—but in its apparent capacity to organize ghetto experience against the bankrupt claims of the official system. As a symbolic representation—a fantasy and a projection—it provides a rationale for the pursuit of African history and culture, for African dress and hair styles, and for the passionate search for history and tradition. If much of that history has to be created or magnified, if petty chiefs are being elevated into great kings, if obscure tinkerers are growing into great scientists, that does not fully cancel the validity of the myth or the needs it fulfills. Rather it enhances them. Every travesty of scholarship conducted in the name of African culture reflects a corresponding travesty in the name of American history and civilization.

At the heart of that mythology, however, lies a naïve faith in some sort of collective identity, and in the magical transformation that will produce it. That faith grows partly out of intimidation—intimidation, that is, by the self-congratulatory declarations of groups which have made it—and partly out of the bewilderment of a misunderstood and largely illusory failure. It assumes, for example, that the Negro is not an American, is indeed not much of anything, a sort of cultural savage who was stripped of his inheritance and given little in return. In its most primitive form—in its blackest versions—the myth depicts the white man as a thief who stole everything he has, whose economic and political power was achieved at the expense of the Negro. The Negro, in other words, was not merely a slave in America, he was the prime source of the white man's wealth. But in seeking to emulate other ethnic groups, even the sophisticated black nationalist who knows economic history better than to ascribe all American wealth to slavery, even he remains the victim of the white man's sociology. The Jews made it—according to the current notion—because they came to America with cultural traditions and an ethnic cohesiveness that provided identity and a basis for collective action. The Negro in this version is still an immigrant; he, too, will make it by reclaiming his immigrant's baggage and starting the process of acculturation all over again. By going back, back, back into some sort of primordial past, into the African kingdoms, to ancient Egypt, even to the beginnings of human life (which, we are now told, can be placed in Africa), the Negro will find himself and achieve the power to be personally and socially effective.

This is confusion confounded. Malcolm never shed his innocent's belief that in some Eastern or African state, in some distant land, men had achieved the ability to live together in harmony without friction or exploitation. His narrative of the royal treatment he received from Arabian sheiks and African politicians is the story of a hustler pushing the golden elixir, a hipster's version of the promised land. In his exotic descriptions of his pilgrimage to the East, there is never a suggestion that Arabia is still a feudal state which exploits its underclass as ruthlessly as any society on earth and whose record of slavery is unmatched in human history. For Malcolm, the Middle East was a blessed society of mutual respect, racial brotherhood, and personal dignity, and American civilization was feudal and corrupt.

The American myth has, in effect, been turned inside out, but it is still the American myth. Malcolm, in his last years, shed his Muslim preoccupations and his mystical racism. But he never resolved his ambiguities about American values. Nor did he fully come to understand either his own Americanism or what it means to be an American Negro. Every black Peace Corps volunteer in Senegal or Tanzania has discovered that in every respect that matters he is not an African come home, but an American abroad. The nationalist still imagines that he can will himself into becoming an African, and that by so doing, he can be what in nineteenth-century romantic thought was described as the American Adam, the new man, free from the corruptions of the old world (then Europe, now America), who, in a new Eden (then America, now a country still to be imagined), could build a world untainted by sin. The African mythology, rather than affirming the Negro's American identity, rather than glorifying it, wants to strip him of it.

The black drive for recognition and the pressure for the institution of black forms—African and American—is riven with inconsistencies and ambiguities. It wants to send the American Negro on two symbolic transatlantic voyages when he probably has no need to make even one. At the same time it is divided between the urge to foster an indigenous Afro-American culture and its passion to give Negroes the power and possibilities to control Western institutions, technology, and culture. To deny anyone the opportunity to learn Swahili may well be parochial or

even racist; but to demand—in the name of Black Power—
that Swahili be taught is to ask a luxury that few people
—white or black—can afford. This is not to say that the
search for the black past and for the legitimate recognition of the black present is worthless. It means only that it
is misdirected and still too much subject to the implications of white supremacy.

What the nationalists want to do with the schools is
simply to replace white boredom with black. They have,
of course, every right to ask for it. It is no more damaging
to fall asleep over Benjamin Banneker, Crispus Attucks,
and the kingdoms of the Nile than it is over Thomas
Edison, Sam Adams, and the tariff of 1820. But in doing
it the nationalists are confusing symbol and substance and
aping those forms and styles that constitute the weakest
elements of the existing system. In one breath they have
declared the prevailing American myth a sham; in the
next they have adopted it, colored it black, and labeled it
good. Scratch African nationalism just a little bit, and it
comes out American: puritanical, messianic, and bourgeois. Deep inside him, Malcolm was a cross between the
Ben Franklin of hard work and thrift, the George F. Bab-
bitt who knew that it paid to advertise, and the Calvinistic
moralist decrying the decline in values. Without knowing
it, Malcolm, too, was a bastard of the West. A school run
largely on his ultimate premises—and there are not likely
to be many—would make any Yankee schoolmaster proud.

Which is not to denigrate the idea of Black Power, but
only to redefine and liberate it from the pursuit of a false
ethnic model. A disproportionate number of Negro intellectuals—and black militants—are bemused by Jews. Because the entire mythology of urban education and ethnic
cohesiveness is saturated with Jewish examples, and because in New York the schools are predominantly Jewish,

that bemusement is understandable. The Jews used the schools, why shouldn't the Negro? The Jews have Israel, why shouldn't the Negroes have Africa? If the Jews relied on their old-world culture to propel them into the mainstream of America, why not the Negroes? The American Negro, in other words, is supposed to turn himself into an African so that he can become a Jew and thereby transform himself into a WASP.

It may well be true that the Jews were more successful than most ethnic groups in using the schools to gain advancement. Yet clearly that success—of whatever degree —was based on the character of the cultural content of Jewish tradition and not simply the existence of a culture. To the extent that they succeeded in the public schools, the Jews—and especially the European Jews—were superbly matched to the demands and style of their teachers and curriculum. The tradition of education, and the respect for teachers and learning was, in most instances, reinforced by the sense of mercantile values. Both coincided with the values and aspirations of the schools. The Jews were qualified bourgeois clients for bourgeois education. That those schools also happened to be Protestant—with "nondenominational" prayers and hymns and Protestant teachers—merely reinforced ethnic and religious cohesiveness and provided enough discrimination to motivate the recruits.

Most other immigrant groups did not use the schools for advancement into the mainstream. Irish or Italian power was exercised through the Church, the political ward, and a vast array of semi- or non-skilled political or commercial occupations, some of them of doubtful legality. Neither the Italians nor the Irish brought any great passion for intellectual attainment. Most of the Italians were southern villagers among whom there was no ideology of change. "Intellectual curiosity and originality were ridi-culed or suppressed," wrote Nathan Glazer in *Beyond the Melting Pot.* " 'Do not make your child better than you are,' runs a south Italian proverb." And while the Irish dutifully sent their children to school (often to parochial school), they rarely expected the school to do much more than enforce standards of discipline, order, and morality.

The historical precedents for Black Power are, there-fore, not educational but political; ethnic pride and co-hesiveness manifested themselves in political activity or in social and commercial associations, but they were antithetical to the educational practices and mythology of the schools. Even when the schools recognized ethnic dis-tinctions, they usually did so in terms of condescending clichés: Italian grocers, Chinese laundrymen, Jewish tailors, and all the rest. In many instances, the best the schools ever did for any real display of cultural individu-ality was to treat it as quaint, and the frequent result was that children of immigrant parents were embarrassed by the customs and manners of their elders.

Black Power, despite its mythological overtones, is more like Irish or Italian power than Jewish power. Though its prime objective in the cities includes the schools, the most immediate results are likely to be political and not educa-tional. What it contains in educational or cultural theory —leaving aside its African mystique—is not very far from the mainstream. At the same time, restoration of some form of the political-ward system (which, after all, is what local control resembles) may be the most effective route of entry into the mainstream. The schools and social services generally (welfare, social work, poverty programs) are the major growth areas in the social economy today.

The claims of black or community power for school control are, needless to say, perfectly legitimate, not because they necessarily promise educational superiority, but because in the American political tradition public institutions are presumably controlled by the people they serve. When a black community leader declares that a particular public school is "our school," he is speaking as an American, not as an educational theorist. To oppose colonialism, after all, is not necessarily to be an African. "We are," said a Negro who was demonstrating for local control, "like Boston Tea Party Indians."

What the black experience can bring to the classroom and to the educational process (in black schools as well as white) is its own passion, its own humanity, its own techniques for survival in a society that threatens increasingly to make a virtue of suffering, or to romanticize the glories of Negro survival under brutalizing conditions. The image of the ubiquitous plantation revolutionary—every man a Nat Turner—is as sentimental as the mythology of the happy slave. Stereotypes, it seems, always tend to breed countertypes. Nonetheless, there is hardly any argument against the assertion—the fact—that the Negro's life in America and his accumulated experience and passions represent something that demands recognition, something that this society and especially its schools desperately need.

The trouble with the conventional school is not its failure to credit the achievements of "great Negroes"—one sees their pictures pinned to every wallboard of every black school in America: King, Thurgood Marshall, Dr. Charles Drew, William H. Hastie, Baldwin—but its failure to recognize the cultural and social importance of the Negro experience. The pictures on the wall (or the names in the book) affirm that a bunch of black guys, given a chance, can do as well as whites in the white man's game. And surely this is important. But perhaps it is equally important—more important—to indicate that some whites, if they work hard at it, are almost as good as blacks as jazz musicians, dancers, athletes, and human beings; that, indeed, there are whites who believe as fervently in justice as blacks. Which is to say that the schools might begin to consider the question of whether the many things to which they now pay only lip service may not be of greater value than the things they actually practice and reward. Where is the school that regards the arts, music, literature on a par with formalized and routinized operations of the three R's, and that upholds the graces of civilized life— good food, good stories, personal and moral courage, and political and legal justice—with the rhetoric of petty bourgeois life: thrift, punctuality, conformity? In this respect, it is not the bourgeois character of the schools that can and should be altered, but their pettiness. What they lack is the sense of high purpose. They suffer, in short, from a historic innocence. Yes, they are out of place, but they are also out of time and out of mind. They exist in a middle world like prisons, police stations, and penal colonies—are, in a sense, part of a world that is neither black nor white, neither modern and technological, nor traditional and humane. If they are irrelevant to the Negro, it is not simply because they are missing the peculiar idiom of the ghetto, because they deal in white picket fences and green lawns while their pupils know only tenements and asphalt. It is because they don't deal in the fundamentals of life at all: birth, death, love, violence, passion; because they don't recognize the mortality or the brevity of human existence; because, in their passion for fundamentals they miss the elemental: the tragic, the heroic, the beautiful, the ugly. And it is in these things that the Negro and his experience may have far more to ask, far more to contribute.

That man [wrote Baldwin] who is forced each day to
snatch his manhood, his dignity, out of the fire of human
cruelty that rages to destroy it, knows if he survives his
effort, and even if he does not survive it, something about
himself and human life that no school on earth—and indeed, no church—can teach.

And indeed, these cannot be taught, they can only be
learned, yet clearly they can be part of the ethos in which
schools and teachers operate. The schools can recognize
that singing the blues is not an aberration, but a universal
condition.

[1969]

THE ROMANTIC CRITICS OF EDUCATION

In the free-for-all of educational commentary, where the half-life of ideas is pitifully short, the ashes of forgotten gods often materialize in the bodies of new critics. Jefferson and Rousseau returned in the form of John Dewey, Pestalozzi in the work of Maria Montessori, and now Dewey himself is reemerging in what is probably the most significant body of educational criticism since World War II. What makes this criticism significant, however, is not its debt to the master but its newness and freshness, and more often than not, its radical refusal to accept the terms of the increasingly sterile debates of the past twenty years.

The new critics—Edgar Z. Friedenberg, Paul Goodman, Jules Henry,° John Holt, and others—are far too independent and cantankerous to develop a consistent voice or anything that could be considered a program, but their common defense of children and adolescents and their fundamental attacks on established practices have given them a place apart from the conventional critics. They have been called romantics, genteel anarchists, and middle-aged adolescents; they have been attacked as anti-intellectuals and hailed as saviors. But for the most part the established leadership of American education has simply ignored them.

In many respects the new critics are more interested in the processes of growing up, in learning and experience, than they are in the formalities of educational programs, the design of curricula or the planning of administrative conveniences. They share with Dewey a faith in the healthy capabilities of children and with Rousseau a belief that "everything is good as it comes from the hands of the Creator: everything degenerates in the hands of man." Holt writes that "nobody is born stupid," that "we encourage children to act stupidly." In their common view a hostile society and its educational system cripple and destroy the processes of learning, the dignity of youth, and the natural instincts of curiosity and self-realization, and they regard schools particularly as coercive instruments designed to enforce conformity and deny self-esteem. Some of their work, and notably Goodman's, contains a sense of loss and a feeling that somewhere in the past the world offered opportunities to the young, that there

° Jules Henry died in 1969.

is no longer any "man's work" to do. For Goodman and some of the others, the society now looks on the young not as individuals but as part of some "national purpose," making them "an exploited and an outcast class."

Although the new critics are all teachers, and are all affiliated with American education, they belong to no establishment or hierarchy, not even to a single kind of institution. Spiritually, and often physically, they are itinerants. Their home, if they have one at all, is the liberal weekly or monthly, the campus lecture platform (often at the invitation of students), and occasionally the scholarly journal. Friedenberg is a sociologist now teaching at the University of California at Davis, Goodman a humanist and novelist who has become a kind of academic traveler, Henry an anthropologist at Washington University (St. Louis), and Holt a teacher in a private secondary school. Nevertheless they share common attitudes derived from their belief that contemporary society and its educational system are hostile to the processes of learning and maturation. Goodman's books *Growing Up Absurd* (1959), *Compulsory Mis-education* (1962), and *The Community of Scholars* (1964); Friedenberg's *Coming of Age in America* (1965) and *The Vanishing Adolescent* (1959); and Henry's *Culture Against Man* (1963) are variations on the theme of alienation, empty conformity and middle-class repression. They are reports on how teachers, guidance counselors, parents, and administrators seduce and coerce children into self-denial, how they teach them games of evasion, and how they deprive them of their desire for honest confrontations with the adult world.

Friedenberg writes in *The Vanishing Adolescent:*

> Adolescent growth can and should lead to a completely human adulthood; defined as a stable sense of self, it could lead nowhere else . . . Youngsters who do not

achieve this stability [are], in a sense, victims of cruelty, misfortune or social pathology . . . But they are also the products of what, in our society, is normal growth; of growth that is consistently distorted so as to lead to the outcome society actually expects, and under ordinary circumstances, rewards. . . . Subjective intensity, disciplined but not repressed, lies at the heart of integrity, of artistic creativity, and of adolescence. It seems to me in the last analysis, that *this* is what terrifies the contemporary middle class most. Any individual through whom subjective intensity may intrude into the processes of bureaucratic equilibrium is extremely threatening to our society.

The argument is that adults fear adolescents, fear their unrepressed instincts and their honest questions—sexual and otherwise—because the adults themselves are too involved in conflicting commitments and ambiguous moral situations. Indeed, it says, contemporary American society simply cannot tolerate the natural humanity of the young. It must therefore confuse and twist it, leaving an accumulation of pathology in its wake. To Goodman, dropouts, delinquents, and college beatniks are all victims of the same process, and have all refused to accept the terms of organized society and the empty rat race (his phrase) which it imposes. Here, as in other ideas, Goodman and Friedenberg borrow a great deal from David Riesman and Erik Erikson, who were among the first to explore the paths of contemporary alienation and conformity. What they add to these ideas, however, is not simply popularization or the optimistic view of human nature derived from Rousseau and Dewey, but also their particular observations of the demands and denials which schools and teachers inflict on the young. They are not interested in test scores, rates of college admission and other ordinary means of evaluation. But they have gone to the classroom and the campus and have chosen to look at things that most teachers and administrators have never seen. They have become adept at analyzing the socio-logical and pedagogical games that schools and teachers play with their students, how they teach children to pre-tend and prevaricate. In *How Children Fail*, Holt con-cludes:

> We have only to convince ourselves that a lie will be "better" for the children than the truth and we will lie. We don't always need even that excuse; we often lie only for our own convenience . . . We present ourselves to children as if we were gods, all-knowing, all-powerful, always rational, always just, always right. This is worse than any lie we could tell about ourselves . . . As we are not honest with them, so we won't let children be honest with us . . . We require them to take part in the fiction that school is a wonderful place and that they love every minute of it. They learn early that not to like school or the teacher is *verboten*, not to be said, not to be even thought.

For Goodman, the whole process of conventional educa-tion is brainwashing:

> The components are a uniform world-view, the absence of any viable alternative, confusion about the relevance of one's own experience and feelings, and a chronic anxiety, so that one clings to the one world-view as the only secur-ity. This *is* brainwashing.

Holt and Jules Henry advance the argument further with their contention that the whole educational process is obsessed with fear. "In order not to fail," says Henry in *Culture Against Man*, "most students are willing to be-lieve anything and not to care whether what they are told is true or false. Thus one becomes absurd through being afraid; but paradoxically, only by remaining absurd can one feel free from fear." When Holt and Henry write that schools teach children to be stupid, they are describing a system that sacrifices curiosity and intelligence to the cause of order and simplicity in classroom management. To cite Henry again: "An intellectually creative child may fail, for example, in social studies, simply because he cannot understand the stupidities he is taught to believe as 'fact.' He may even end up agreeing with his teachers that he is 'stupid' in social studies. Learning in social studies is, to no small extent . . . learning to be stupid. The child with a socially creative imagination will not be encouraged to play among new social systems, values and relationships; nor is there much likelihood of it, if for no other reason than that the social studies teachers will perceive such a child as a poor student."

Friedenberg, who sees conventional education in highly sophisticated terms, and who is considerably less prone to polemics than most of the others, describes the school —and especially the high school—as a great engine functioning to obfuscate the human instincts and moral quests of the young. The school is more interested in good public relations, administrative convenience and political peace than it is in the growth of its students. Thus, instead of confronting the problems of students directly, it denies or evades them, teaching its students that "they can only win esteem by how they look and behave, not for what they are. . . . It is more firmly convinced than ever that its job is to teach youngsters to respond to other people's expectations. While it emphasizes the expression of personality, it conveys to the student that personality should be built on certain standard plans, superficially varied according to taste, and that expression should consist of a fairly continuously emitted code signal by which other persons can recognize what they want when they see it.

If they don't want it, there must be something wrong with either the personality or the signal, and it must be changed." In such a system even the rebelliousness of the lower-class youngster is quickly crushed: "These youngsters are handy with their fists and worse: but they are helpless in the meshes of middle-class administrative procedure and are rapidly neutralized and eliminated by it . . . They quickly learn that the most terrifying creatures are those whose bite passes unnoticed at the time and later swells, festers and paralyzes; they cannot defend themselves against the covert, lingering hostility of teachers and school administrators." The school, in brief, becomes a production plant turning out shoddy goods for the dime-store trade; its teachers are not professionals but petty civil servants; and guidance counselors, far from helping, generally operate as the agents of a "Ministry of Adjustment." The school denies students the right to go to the john without a pass, the privilege of determining how they will cut their hair or wear their clothes, even the honor of direct personal punishment:

> What has been violated is not so much freedom as dignity. I do not mean simply that somebody has been unnecessarily rude—quite the opposite. Assaults on dignity are usually very friendly and well meaning—that is part of the strategy. But the action taken has been basically contemptuous of students, negligent of their real characteristics as human beings and indifferent to their needs and feelings as individuals. In the blandest possible way, they have been pushed around. They have been pitted against one another in strategically organized committees, seduced with little awards for leadership and contributions to school life; taught gamey old political tricks for ensuring the triumph of good government; playfully spanked for displaying undue and unreasonable ardor. If this is not enough, playfulness abruptly ceases and is replaced by

pious sorrow that heedless young people are ruining their chances with their record in school. The record is being very carefully kept.

The arguments of the new critics take them into territory in which most other educational commentators fear to tread. By recognizing schools and colleges as agents of a society that is seriously maladjusted to human purposes, if not altogether sick, they attack the institutions not because they fail the purposes of the order, but because they are too successful. Goodman and Friedenberg are both critics of the leveling effect of a system of education motivated and operated by the middle class that denies true distinction by pretending it doesn't exist, and they conclude by questioning the system itself. Goodman assigns the ultimate responsibility to a bureaucratic, warfare-oriented state that demands recruits to help make it function; Friedenberg places it in the insecurity of the lower-middle class which staffs the schools and remains their chief influence. But both see the consequences in the same light and, independently, they arrive at similar sets of recommendations. Because the schools are destructive not only of genuine learning and academic quality, but also of personal dignity, they serve only the goals of an unhealthy social order and not the human purposes toward which education is presumably directed. Would it therefore not be better to abandon compulsory public education altogether in favor of a far more diversified set of voluntary opportunities ranging from apprentice trade programs to high-quality boarding schools for rich and poor students? Would it not be preferable to make all education voluntary, for—in Goodman's words—"no growth to freedom occurs except by intrinsic motivation"? In urging these arguments both Goodman and Friedenberg raise issues that not long ago would have been considered simply undiscussible. To question the validity of the American system of democratic education was like spitting on the flag, and any individual caught suggesting that it be broken up was immediately stripped of his credentials as a responsible critic.

Because of their inescapable radicalism and their assault on the absurdity of the conditions of growing up, Goodman, Holt, and the others have pejoratively been dubbed romantics (i.e., soft-headed). If the society has to be reconstituted before education can become a viable human enterprise, or if the school system has to be torn apart, then the whole argument can be dubbed as the work of a collection of dreamers. But what was unthinkable a few years ago has started to look only visionary in 1967. The obvious educational failures of the past few years, the crash programs of compensatory education, the Head Starts, the dropout centers, the Job Corps programs already indicate that at least when it comes to its most obvious problems, the society may be ready to go beyond the traditional program of the public schools to avert total catastrophe. It has become clear, moreover, that the demonstrations at Berkeley and elsewhere reflect serious discontent among undergraduates with the way conventional academic institutions—and the society beyond—have treated their students. Goodman has, in great measure, become the spokesman of the alienated and the rebellious, and he has become a sort of roving prophet for the independent students who are establishing free universities and similar para-academic organizations. Thus the pejorative description of Goodman and others as romantics has required at least the qualifications that the size of his following makes mandatory.

But the sobriquet "romantic" nevertheless holds true in Goodman's sentimental regard for the relations and significance of a community of citizens that ceased to exist with the passing of the nineteenth-century village and a community of scholars not seen since the Middle Ages. Where will we find the kind of productive employment that qualifies as "man's work"? How will we manage the power of contemporary technology without the bureaucracies to manage them? How will we operate successful universities of independent scholars without administrators, presidents, and trustees? It is, after all, very difficult to construct a Boeing 707 in one's basement; Goodman, in some of his campus talks, has spoken about apprenticing young men to small printers (where, like Ben Franklin, they can learn a trade and simultaneously become literate), but where are the small printers, and what can one learn on a hand press that will be useful on a high-speed, automated machine that can turn out thirty thousand impressions in an hour? Goodman himself acknowledges that his liberalism has taken him fairly close to the radical right, but the sentimental regard for the virtues of an agrarian society that he shares with some of the people who call themselves "conservatives" is no more relevant when it comes from him than when it originates with Barry Goldwater.

It is Goodman's apparent unwillingness to come to terms with the demands of the technological culture that has earned him and some of his philosophical brothers the label "anti-intellectual." His chief villains—men like James B. Conant—are people who see education as training ground for the demands that this culture makes: they accept those demands while Goodman appears reluctant to have anything to do with them. But the charge confuses the issue because it rides roughshod over Goodman's sense that the mind is being harnessed to organizational demands like a computer, instead of being left unfettered to work out the development of civilized possibilities. What is not clear is how that is possible *before* the social managers have learned to operate and control the technological and bureaucratic structures with which we all have to live.

More important, perhaps, is the vagueness of the remedy. The strength of the new critics lies in their ability to see the educational process as part of a coherent system that involves not only the schools but the general demands of the social order. But if the whole society is unbalanced, where do you find the lever and fulcrum to move it? While Goodman has become an accurate prophet of the ailments of the alienated students, his message, in their mouths, has as often as not become no more than an agonized wail. To act at all, in such a situation, is to deny the universal hopelessness of the whole thing, and to trade your alienation for commitment, thereby denying the premise on which you act. And what of the committed— students who do have programs and who generally hold the philosophical esteem of the new critics? They, after all, are also products of the educational system. The social activists of Students for a Democratic Society, the Peace Corps volunteers, the campus rebels—they all attended the schools and colleges that Friedenberg, Holt, Henry, and Goodman have so effectively described. The irony of the romanticism in the message of people like Goodman is that students may be able to play the game of rebellion just as effectively as they play the game of acquiescence; frustrated creativity can be thrown up to a demanding teacher just as easily as resignation, and chaotic incoherence can be disguised in the garb of self-expression. Friedenberg himself acknowledges that the students may be more implicated in the process—not as victims, but as protagonists—than he had supposed when he wrote *The Vanishing Adolescent* in the late fifties. The book, he says, "pictures the young as engaged in a gallant if hopeless struggle with the timidity and corruption of the adult world, usually in the person of school officials; it would have been more accurate to picture American youth rather as already deeply implicated in the deeds and values of their culture. Mostly they go along with it and sincerely believe that in doing so they are putting down trouble-makers and serving the best interests of their community." What this argument represents, clearly, is a realization that even the kids are not free of original sin, and an understanding of the ubiquity of the problem. It suggests that children also can be nasty little rascals, and that some of those finky juveniles scrambling up the ladder of success aren't just doing it because somebody else is pushing. This is what makes Friedenberg a more sophisticated writer than those of his fellows who see the whole business as a conspiracy of the old against the young.

The observations of the new critics take them to what is essentially an elitist position. They are, ultimately, critics of the techniques and attitudes that the liberals and progressives worked out thirty years ago. What they attack is what democratic education *turned out to be.* It is directed not at John Dewey or at Jefferson but at the corruptions established in their name. Goodman describes how the student liberties at the University of Virginia, which had been meant by Jefferson to be gentlemanly and revolutionary "have come to a tight little code, prohibiting walking on the lawn and regulating the nuances of getting drunk . . ." Dewey's notion to train people through actual experience, to learn by doing, "was entirely perverted. The conservatives and the businessmen cried out and the program was toned down. The practical training and community democracy, whose purpose was to live scientifically and change society was changed into 'socially useful' subjects and a psychology of 'belonging.'" Using a different set of terms, Holt and Friedenberg describe the perversion as the replacement—under corrupted Deweyan impulses—of manipulation for coercion. "The would-be progressives thought," says Holt, "that there were good ways and bad ways to coerce children (the bad ones mean harsh, cruel, the good ones gentle, persuasive, subtle, kindly), and that if they avoided the bad and stuck to the good they would do no harm." Because the traditional dealt with masses of children, says Henry, it could only manage by reducing them all to a common definition. Thus it created, in his words, "the essential nightmare" which had to be dreamed to provide the fears necessary to drive people from failure to success. The modern school is a response to this nightmare, providing fun and impulse release, and a bland emptiness in place of the traditional obsessions. Thus contemporary educators are unable to understand that "a vital democracy can be the product of a disciplined and intelligent population only; that disorder and laxity are poison to democracy." Friedenberg is far more sympathetic to the elitist pretensions of college fraternities, for example, than to the middle-class liberals who would make them accessible to all; and he respects the aristocratic orientations of prep schools far more than the bland management of the typical middle-class public high school. "I am not seeking to eliminate privilege, but to create it and distribute it more intelligently," he writes in *Coming of Age in America*. "I am not trying to be fair, or to identify and reward the most deserving, but to find educational means for sponsoring and nurturing more trustworthy and humane people than those among whom our lives now seem destined to be spent, and spent utterly." This is a worthy cause, but it is also a risky one. For thousands of years people have struggled against those who claimed to be more trustworthy and humane, and who oppressed others in the name of culture and civility.

But that is not to disparage either the wish or the possibilities that it may produce. The fact that the schools reflect perfectly the society that produced them is not necessarily justification for the perpetual maintenance of either. And clearly the vague oppressiveness of the order demands not less diversification, not fewer distinctions, but more: it is only when the distinctions and the diversification exist that any genuine humanity is possible. Almost every sympathetic critic concedes that what went wrong with Jefferson and Dewey was not the ideal but the execution: to be a democrat and to believe in individual fulfillment is the very antithesis of being a leveling apostle of homogenization. And if the failures of the Deweyan utopia ought to teach the advocates of new utopias some humility, there is no reason why the corruptions and degradations of our status-conscious technological wonderland should be immune from the commentary they deserve.

If nothing else, people like Friedenberg have raised the level of the current discourse from its programmatic, managerial plateau to a level where individual human beings are restored to the argument. The passions that followed Sputnik and the college panic divided us between those who wanted to make education a more efficient training instrument for the Cold War and middle-management, and those who resisted because the pap of life adjustment was more comfortable than intellectual rigor. The new critics have reminded us—sometimes, albeit, with too much wail—that relevant education has little to do with either, and that if it does not deal with the humanity of its students, it is not dealing with anything.

[1967]

THE SCHOOLMASTERS

Most of it is familiar: Harvard types in cord suits, sweating in the 100-degree heat like ordinary mortals; a couple of shrinks; a rabbi from Cleveland; Louis Harris with the poll data; a guru from the music industry in a $300 suit playing Bob Dylan and Simon and Garfunkel records; Paul Goodman with his shirt-tail out; David Riesman with the generation gap; Jerry Avorn, last year's editor of the *Columbia Spectator;* a dozen or so high school students (rural North Carolina and Central Harlem, fancy prep and small-town high); some eighty public school administrators of the Advanced

Administrative Institute of the Harvard Graduate School of Education—deputy superintendents from big cities; full-dress, four-star supers from Edina and Shaker Heights, from Salamanca and Canton; plus a few monsignors—diocesan school superintendents—doing summer business in polo shirts.

The topic is like the cast, like the set, like the heat: The Youth Revolution. (The coming insurrection in the high school? The new culture? Why kids hate school? Hypocrisy among the aged?) But when Harvard calls, people come—even in July. The Advanced Administrative Institute at Harvard is an annual affair for experienced school personnel, but this particular meeting has more urgency, allows far less time, than the normal conference dealing with the mysteries of mustering support for bond issues or the problems of getting along with the school board. The Youth Revolution is more than rhetoric, more than a fabrication of newspaper pundits and cheap sociologists. But what are the connections between that revolution—whatever it may be—and the schools? Do the people who run those schools feel they have a problem, and in what way do they regard it as something that relates to what they do? Can "the problem" be administered away with a few new tactics, or does it reflect pervasive inadequacies in the society and the educational system? Those who come to Harvard are touted high on the with-it-ness scale. If they don't know, who does?

The heat is a symbolic equalizer. For much of the time we are all incarcerated in un-air-conditioned buildings that impose an elusive atmospheric democracy. Some of the superintendents are wearing Bermuda shorts and sandals, all the duds that violate the dress code of Central High; out of uniform, they, too, are ordinary mortals, middle-aged men, some of them going to pot, trying to

figure what the hell it's all about, or maybe trying to figure
a way not to have to figure at all. In the dormitory, the
kids are playing hard rock, some of them dancing, some
of them playing cards with a young priest-administrator
from Chicago, others rapping with a black administrator
from New York. Equality in the hot living room of Holmes
Hall at Radcliffe. "This whole damn thing," says the way-
out with the extra-length hair, "is like a Green Beret
counterinsurgency manual. They're trying to figure what
color hats the guerrilla leaders will wear."

Maybe, for some it is. Maybe for most. There is a recent
copy of *School Management* magazine floating around:
STRATEGIES FOR COPING WITH BOYCOTTS, VIOLENCE, SIT-INS.
In *School Management*, the kids are the enemy, barbarian
hordes who have to be conned, or co-opted, or accommodated. Success is to get the kids "back into class in short
order." But what about the other guys? What about the
guy from the Midwestern city—a deputy superintendent
—who confesses that two thirds of the high schools in his
district stink and that the kids are perfectly right to
scream about teachers who can't teach, administrators
who are inaccessible, and programs from another age and
frame of mind? Is there a sensitivity scale? Here are the
men who supposedly run a cross section of American
schools, ghetto schools and suburban schools, and all-
American mainstream schools in places like Sioux Center,
Iowa, and Franklin Lakes, New Jersey. How many of
them expect to do business as usual next year and forever after? There were high school student demonstrations and protests last year: some in New York City,
others in New Jersey, Ohio, Florida, and Minnesota; and
no one can really conceive of what normalcy might again
be like, even if he fell over it in the lunchroom. We all
(let's not say all; say many of us) sense that something

is about to happen, that 1969-70 is going to be the year of Central High the way that 1968-69 was the year of Harvard, Cornell, and San Fran State. (And perhaps it will be the year of the junior high, too.) Race, pot, music, the anger of youth—all the elements are there. And so is business-as-usual. Six hours a day of incarceration, thirty kids to a class, listening to a drone; guidance counselors advising independence, while the teachers sniff the john for smoke; hall passes and after-school detention; phony student councils and pompous principals issuing the daily homily. They are masters of the put-down, experts in condescension. "What they're doing," says a tough, angry man from the Minneapolis schools, "is killing kids."

Everybody is trying to tell them something, and after a few days the message ought to be deafening. At a moment like this, only a boob could worry about the school bonds: Mary McCarthy, Radcliffe senior and daughter of Senator Eugene McCarthy, telling them, with four-letter words and other appropriate shorthand, that kids have lost faith in the ordinary institutions of society; Julius Hobson, who beat the track system in the Washington schools and who is now an angry minority on the district school board, speaking about the society's war on the young, about dirty old men who worry about mini-skirts and see-through blouses instead of concerning themselves with racial injustice and the education of children; kids telling about harassment by cops and administrators (and other kids describing how, at sixteen, they are being pursued by white vigilantes, or Black Panthers, or dope pushers); conservative kids and radical kids and moderate kids trying to say that at least part of the time schools are irrelevant, stupid, and repressive.

The messages are so thick that the overload of noise becomes itself an element of administrative relief. (Thank

God, says the secret heart in the big office, the kids can't agree. The enemy is divided.) For the first few days of the institute, the kids—despite their divergent views about politics and race—form a phalanx, a defensive clot against Authority in Superior Numbers. "We stick together, stick up for each other, even if we don't agree," says one, but he cannot explain what they have in common other than age. (Later, he will begin to learn.) But the divisions become apparent, almost chaotic, when the kids sit down, all of them, around a table without a moderator or even a working microphone. For an hour and a half, the irrationalities and the hard facts of diverse and often bitter experience are tossed, inconsistent and incomplete, at the visiting Romans. The kids dredge up the phrases of hand-me-down pop sociology, stuff about "elitist theory" and "multiple value systems" (reminder: only a couple are over eighteen; a few are barely sixteen). There are references to FBI conspiracies, to Harvard's use of its investments ("Harvard," says one, "could buy South Africa if it wanted to"—but he neglects to mention that across the street an all-white construction crew is erecting a new dormitory for the girls of Radcliffe), to Black Panthers and the SDS, to the use of mace-spraying helicopters on the Berkeley campus, to the brutalities of ghetto schools and the injustices of racism, to nonviolent and violent revolution. The leader of an organization of American Indian students reproaches the other kids for shooting off their mouths, making social causes of their paranoia, without having an idea of what they really want. The Indian is tough and cool, like Cochise in a John Ford movie. ("White man talk too much, white man afraid.") The students—from black Harlem militant to Midwest racist—are expected to set out a bill of particulars for the Youth Revolution; instead they set forth a still-incoherent set of attitudes that reflect precisely the diversities for which they were chosen in the first place. If you bring together an alienated long-haired militant from the suburbs and future ROTC captains from North Carolina, you can't really expect them to agree on whether schools, courts, and policemen collude to harass students, on the imminence of revolution, or on the racial inequities in American life.

After all that, the kids were patsies for the put-down, patronizing, fake-sympathetic, the voices of reflection impressed by "these young people," the tone of the high school principal after the assembly discussion program. New England monsignor: "If such young people are coming out of our high schools we must be doing something right." Prep school dean, cultivated, mini-Ivy masculinity: "Admire your honesty . . . but . . . you have to ask yourself what you've made of your opportunities." Superintendent from Midwest suburb: "There's still some tact, courtesy, and good manners to be learned. . . . Youth still tends to violence. . . . Good manners are essential to good communication." There was a lot of palaver about how the kids hadn't used Roberts's *Rules of Order*, how it took them too long to establish some form of parliamentary procedure, how their language offended nice people; and before the palaver was over, the kids were on the defensive. Some of them vaguely realized it, but for most, the technique was so much a part of habitual experience that it went unnoticed. "They just refuse to listen to what's being said," one of them complained later. What the superintendents had done—not all, but many—was to prove that open-mindedness was, like everything else, a good ploy.

It was, of course, not unanimous. There was an angry minority who knew what had happened. "Three fourths of these guys," said a man from the Midwest, "don't have a clue." "You bet we have a problem," said another, a man responsible for his system's "human relations" efforts. "We should have known all the things the kids are demanding of us, but we messed up our opportunities for reform. The students demanded we fire a principal who was inaccessible, and that we do something about what they considered—rightly so—a watered-down program. But I'm not sure we can act." In his schools, the Mexican-Americans are taking action to demand community control, and the white vigilantes (students), the Nazis, and the Panthers are all organized. There have been bombings, riots, and several deaths, but the human relations man—no angry young upstart—is still a minority. Few others, in his system, feel any urgency about the problem.

Among the administrators at Harvard who had faced protests or violence, there was talk about outside agitators, and even more talk about faint remedies: individualized instruction and a little black history for race riots, smaller classes for cultural gaps that had yet to be appreciated or understood. "I don't think we'll have real trouble in Maryland," said another educational statesman. "Maybe some sporadic incidents. . . . The students who are here showed today that they have disagreements, too. So far they just stuck together, but today they showed that they have sharp differences." (Relief.) If there was no real trouble, then obviously there was no real problem.

One night they held up the mirror: Fred Wiseman's documentary film *High School,* photographed in a thoroughly middle-class Philadelphia high school (where local citizens obtained a court injunction to prevent it from being shown); one hour and twenty minutes of boredom, mindlessness, and hypocrisy of decent people. Schoolmarm reading *Casey at the Bat* to a class of blank faces; school disciplinarian telling a kid that the way to be a man was to accept his punishment even though it might be unjust; the Mickey Mouse of "simulated space flight" in a hand-me-down NASA capsule; the baldhead in the corridors asking every living creature, "Where's your pass?"; the well-meaning young thing turning Simon and Garfunkel song lyrics into an English-class exercise as inspiring as scanning the lines of *Hiawatha;* the final irony of the principal reading a letter from a recent graduate who expected to be killed in Vietnam and expressed his gratitude to the school by leaving his insurance money to the scholarship fund. "I'm just a body," he wrote in ultimate tribute to his education, "doing a job."

Did they recognize themselves? Some surely did. ("The film hurt," said a man from Kansas City.) One of the superintendents unintentionally confessed all to a student: "He asked," said the kid, "how it could ever be different with the people they got. I told him he was supposed to be the educator, that it was for him to figure out." There were several men who decided that it was time they listened to their students a little more, one of them a central city administrator of a parochial system who hoped he could get his principals to pay a little attention to what the students were trying to tell them. One of the students—one of the few who had missed the point of the film—later wondered aloud whether the soldier in Vietnam had been killed on his mission. "He was already dead," said an angry administrator from Minneapolis, perhaps one of the most perceptive people there. "And what's more," he said, turning to the student, "you're dead, too."

A few simply denied all. A suburban superintendent from Michigan declared that there were always good teachers and bad ones, and that Wiseman's film had shown only the bad. Many, if you asked them, denied that any of it was accurate; too much was made, they said, of the ugly faces and mannerisms of the school staff. (Earlier one of the students had pointed out that those were precisely the things kids saw all day, that this was a film from the students' point of view. "Actually," she said, "the film was gentle.") Most of the superintendents didn't say anything. Perhaps later they would recognize things at home they had never recognized before. Perhaps. For the moment one could only imagine that full recognition would have been too much, that it would be too destructive, too much a confrontation with what may be, for most, an unalterable reality.

What became clear was that the schoolmen were as much as the kids—perhaps more—prisoners of the system. The shared heat and sweat were indeed symbolic. Most of the superintendents could no more change the fundamental conditions of life in Central High than they could cool off Holmes Hall. (Not only was their political power limited; their imagination was even more circumscribed, and their capacity for anger invisible.) Of all their little hypocrisies—their rhetoric about responsibility and due process, about independence and hard work—none was as great as the pretense that they could, if persuaded, do something to reform things, that they were ethically or intellectually equipped to act.

In the film, one of the students describes his school as a moral and social garbage can: those who preached the virtues within it had never demonstrated (and perhaps knew they never could demonstrate) their capacity to practice them. Even among the more sensitive administrators (save only a very few), the things that were regarded as the legitimate claims of the students simply became the demands of another interest group, a new entry into the bargaining relationship with the teachers' union, the school board, and the PTA. A good superin-

tendent, in that sense, was primarily a skillful and sympathetic negotiator who maintained conditions of trust
so that the bargaining process would never collapse—not a
man who brought fundamental convictions of his own to
bear on the system. (Those who spoke loudest about convictions were almost inevitably educational reactionaries.)
It was nice if the students were pushing since that would
help him push someone else. Little was ever said about
the more fundamental inadequacies of the schools. If the
film was accurate, said a deputy superintendent, then the
only way to improve the schools was to tear the system
apart and start all over again. And that, for most, was
beyond their most ambitious capacities. It was unthinkable.

There was something else, too, something perhaps even
more significant, and that was the moral and cultural
cataclysm that gave the whole gathering its inadequate
name: The Youth Revolution. It was there all over, like
one of those hidden faces in the drawing of the tree. It
was not that the kids had The Word; no one had it. Indeed, the pieties from the kid-lovers were as unbearable
as those of the authoritarians. (What was fascinating about
that was that the once-radical criticism of people like
Goodman and Edgar Friedenberg had gone mainstream
and was now coming back, in garbled form—for public
consumption—from people like Neil Sullivan, the Massachusetts Commissioner of Education.) Perhaps the whole
thing was beyond the forms of conventional analysis, beyond anything that could be said about the lyrics (or even
the music) of the Beatles or the chemistry and sociology
of drugs, about Vietnam, or the draft, or the news media,
or the new technologies. It was surely beyond management; perhaps it was also beyond reason. All those things
are surely involved, but they are no more helpful than a

description of the parts of the elephant for a blind man. The kids certainly did not agree on any of the issues that might be discussed in the Youth Forum, yet they somehow shared a sixth sense—almost a scent—that only they, and no adult, seemed to recognize. Instinctively they knew how grownups (and especially schoolmen) behave; sometimes they accepted it, even liked it; the grownups had no such instincts for the behavior of the kids.

But it went—and goes—even beyond that. Harvard, after all, is no island. The problems that remained inchoate in Cambridge are hardly unique to schools. At some point in the last generation the adults lost their sense of moral security—the whole nation lost it; if they are at all sensitive, the adults know they are whistling in the dark. All the things that once held the schools together—belief in equality, opportunity, independence—have been thrown into doubt as educational or social realities. Whatever assurance we had in World War II began to go with Hiroshima. Jeff Nuttall, in the one really impressive book about the generations (*Bomb Culture*, published in 1969), wrote:

> We knocked out the second enemy (by no means such a discernible villain as Hitler, whom we could easily condemn through the sensational shock of the concentration camps and the obvious poisonous violence of his rhetoric) by alienating all those values we had confirmed in the first victory [Europe]. We had espoused a continuum that negated (running parallel to) the continuum of society. We had espoused an evil as great as the Nazi genocide, we had espoused the instrument for the termination of our benevolent institution, society, and our certain identity, human. We had espoused a monstrous uncertainty both of future and of morality. If, besides the "Nazi gangsters," we were also wrong, who was ever right? If no one was right, what was right, and was right anyway relevant, and

what could guide us through the terrifying freedom such a concept offered? Whatever the answer, it had best be a good one, for we could not rely on ourselves any more than the little yellow man or the evil Hun. . . . The first victory was a victory confirming our merits and security. The second destroyed them irrevocably.

Nuttall divides the generations between those who reached puberty before Hiroshima and those who reached it after, between those who must pretend that the war ended in virtue and who were "incapable of conceiving of life *without* a future"—and those incapable of conceiving life *with* a future. The older group had learned to fake it, the younger generation found them out. ("Dad was a liar. He lied about the war and he lied about sex.") Whether the distinctions are all that simple—Nuttall's, by the way, is not a simple book—it is clear that it isn't just the kids who are challenging established and cherished values, but the adults who have either given them up or betrayed them. Along with the burdens of Hiroshima, Vietnam, and racial injustice, came a growing sense (among the sensitive) that everything that is white, Western, Christian, and rational—everything that once certified superior Culture and Civilization—is in doubt. (Undoubtedly the kids have the initiative, and are, willy-nilly, beginning to set the style. The wardens are prisoners in their own institutions. But there isn't—at least in the kids' minds—all that much to knock over.) The schools, of course, had never been too strong on Culture anyway. Culture with a capital C worked only as the possession of an elite, as a clubby mystery, a common language which originated in the communion of class and social standing, and not in the mysterious processes of the academy. Nonetheless, the fact that Culture existed somewhere was probably enough. Even if the superintendent was more of a Rotarian than a scholar he could still rely on the fact that what his English teacher was doing was certified not only by the values of the counting house, but also by the tradition of Milton and Shakespeare.

He can rely no more. Perhaps more than anyone else, he and his system are the victims of the failure of liberalism and "reason" in America. What, asked Julius Hobson, can a man do for equality and quality in education after he has been to the school board, to the courts, to Congress, and after he has spent a protester's time in jail? His own cause, he told the superintendents, is "equal education or equal chaos." Who will respond to that? For the superintendents, there is no clear signal from anyone, either in the community or the nation at large. There are repetitions of the old rhetoric, hard work, ambition, and much noise about technology and preparation for the world of the future (which are themselves calls to bring the deviants into line), but the rhetoric begins to be less persuasive: fewer students are listening to it, and a growing minority is not listening at all.

There are all sorts of notions of what the school should be, but none of them is possible of realization under existing circumstances. Educational philosophy can have no life of its own, cannot exist without a more general idea of culture or an antecedent political theory, and without a society that practices, rather than betrays, its articulated convictions about peace, freedom, and independence. Any school person who blindly represents the authority and compromises of the community has no reason to expect the full trust of his students. Any school person who professes interest in students and ships them off to Vietnam on the day they graduate is a person whose motives are necessarily in doubt.

There is no general idea of culture in America at this

moment; we are living in a no man's land labeled "the generation gap" which gives its educational system no cues—other than unprincipled conformity—to follow. The school manager of the old style is a lost man charged with the resolution of problems and conflicts he cannot possibly handle or even confront. What distinguishes him from his students is that they are beginning to understand his pathetic weakness, and to discover that he, by all that keeps him together and sane, must forever deny it.

[1969]

THE END OF THE GREAT TRADITION

Higher education has gone mainstream, the old distinctions have vanished, one can no longer determine where "higher education" ends and the rest of the world begins: peripatetic professors, government contracts, political students. The 1960's represented the last decade of the traditional rhetoric about the enterprise: Was the institution public or private? How many students were enrolled? What was the student-faculty ratio? How much student power should there be in university government? What was the proper "role" (God help us) of the university? We're going to look back a few years from now and think, How quaint, how naïve. Many of us will hope that nobody remembers the vast amount of nonsense we published about what's bugging the students, or how we could be "relevant," or how we could combine "breadth with depth." What we are going to ask—if we still have a voice to do so—is whether it is possible to organize knowledge and understanding in such a way as to keep all of education, indeed all of society, from being divided between the emotional and the technical, between mystics and tinkerers.

The division is not between Snow's two cultures, or students versus faculty (or administration) or even the generation gap. (Does the gap move as we all get older, or do people leap over it?) The point is whether the idea of discipline—the way we used to talk about literature or history or mathematics—still makes sense or whether all education will be devoted either to technical questions (the building of economic models, or conflict resolution, or molecular biology) or to such questions as "Who am I?" and "How can I touch you?" For the radicals, the rallying cries are relationship, and confrontation, and engagement, and doing your own thing. Computers do the reasoning and human beings *feel*. Does the book enable you to control spirits, like Prospero? Hell, no. The book enslaves, entraps, deludes, equivocates. "I don't want to read Augustine," says the kid to the professor, "because I don't like Augustine." The kid is a feeler. He already *knows*—doesn't want to know anything more. History is not his bag; history is a cop-out. He knows what's it's like. He has the true faith. He is not merely a romantic; he has flipped back to sixth-century mysticism.

Don't blame him, or consider him as an example of "students" or the "young." By now the star professor is back on the plane, off to do a little consulting or to check with the Institute of Applied Linguistics. The other students are grinding out the papers, or maybe trying to figure out how to put experience into machines, or what conflict resolution has to do with poverty in Harlem. And everybody feeling guilty about feeling, or else proud that they feel more than anybody else. It is not the young against the old, but of young *and* old knowing where to go, how to keep abstraction from running away with passion, and vice versa.

A few years ago Jacques Barzun declared that the liberal arts college is dead or dying because the high school had co-opted the first two years (general education) and the graduate school the last two (specialization). What he should have said is that the liberal arts are dead or dying not because literature or history aren't being taught, but because the common cultural assumptions in which they were rooted have been shattered. We have talked for years about the fact that the ideal of the Renaissance man was unattainable. Leibniz, it has been said, was probably the last man to know everything; we know about the explosion of knowledge and all that. The point, however, is more significant. We have begun to lose faith in rational possibilities. Knowing we can't know, we have given up trying. The questions therefore are technical and the culture existential. The way to the frontier is a narrow path through the jungle. The way to establish one's sense of himself is by way of emotional sensibilities. "I feel, therefore I am." The dilemma is real. The problem is not merely that a few professors have sold out to the Defense Department, the CIA, or the corporations, or that students are obstreperous or slovenly or weak from pot. The problem is that lacking common cultural assumptions—about freedom or religion or the good life—there is no common ground for discourse.

Let's be absolutely clear about this. The university was founded on Renaissance assumptions even if, as in America, it often became a vocational institution. The Renaissance assumptions were fairly simple, even after we had discovered (surely also a Renaissance kind of word) that nobody could know all about everything: belief in reason, a sense that the world—the world of God and man—was knowable, that the *terra incognita* of whatever sort would eventually be explored, that there were certain universal principles and that "culture" was a unitary concept, not something that changed as one hopped from place to place or continent to continent. Yes, there were "higher" and "lower" cultures, but always on a linear scale with ourselves somewhere near the top. The Chinese were highly civilized while the West was still in the "dark ages" (catch them loaded words) because the Chinese had invented gunpowder—wasn't that an achievement? And among the highest of the cultures was, naturally, the German, with Beethoven and Goethe and Schiller. But all of that evaporated at Auschwitz and Dachau, along with some of our self-assurance, when we had finally absorbed the impact of Hiroshima. Slaveholders, imperialists, repressors, the white devil, that's us. Who's to know what's good and for whom? Do your own thing, because only you know. We used to call it anti-intellectualism.

Surely these are extremes, minorities, and all that. But just as surely, the problem is to tame and reform the disciplines, to keep every field in some realm between applied mathematics or symbolic logic and some form of narcissistic breast-beating. Here are all these sophisticated people who've analyzed the world to death, whose whole sense of themselves as intellectuals is a critical sense, arriving at a point where the wisest men are tinkerers, and where the tinkerers earn all the rewards. The student radicals weren't revolting merely against the institution or even against the faculty, but against a system in which all of society, including the majority of students, were involved. The universities, let's face it, haven't been standing in the way of the educational demands of most undergraduates; they've been delivering. The majority— the business students, the ed students, the engineers and agronomists and dental technicians—have been *using* the system to get the emoluments. The disaffected, most of them humanists and social scientists, have been engaging in a kind of status revolt (as the Progressives once did against the industrial robber barons) to keep the university from being used that way. Give the students, *all* the students, full power to determine the curriculum, and it won't take long before they establish something remarkably similar to what they already have.

It is probably for this reason that debates about "relevance" are confusing. There's plenty of relevance in balancing books, learning to run computers, and nuclear physics. What's irrelevant is the liberal arts. (By this time, of course, many of the traditional liberal-arts subjects— mathematics, political science, economics, psychology, the foreign languages—have become vocational; many of those who study them are, in some sense, already on the job.) The subjects appear under the old names in the catalogue, but they involve—or rather should involve—new questions, new sorts of activities, and bear a different relationship to the rest of the world. It is not simply that the professor is interested in his research, or not interested in anything but apprentices and disciples for his own field (although that is a common source of student complaint), it is also that learning has lost its mystery. The traditional liberal-arts program (indeed, the traditional university) was something for a small minority, usually an elite, that was being "educated," and hence initiated, into the temple. Rank and position were not derived from learning, but learning justified them. The doctor from the university was no more able to command spirits than the cobbler, but he thought he could. The common culture was therefore not only small, but its Latin hocus-pocus provided the happy illusion that it was learning, rather than the shared attitudes of a class, which made discourse possible and allowed the world to revolve in its orderly circuit.

The illusion of magic evaporated when the club became too big. Teach an ordinary seaman to use a sextant and he begins to lose respect for the officers; now he, too, can determine where the hell he is. At the same time, either the status of officer starts to lose its glow or the search begins for a new way to pull rank. Hence the rush for new problems, new specialists, new techniques. The growth of knowledge may be a cultural imperative—and it may make life better for us in the long run—but the solution of problems, and the imagination to distinguish the significant from the trivial, is still a matter of individual choice. The production of silly papers is no more defensible than the manufacture of useless gadgets, though it is often rationalized with the same sort of argument. The pressure to publish is illiberal, not only because it steals time from the students, but also because it forces the professors to become technicians. Hence the trip to the Institute of Applied Linguistics. In a system where there are only a handful of real doctors (of English or history or whatever) the holders of chairs can afford to be liberal, can take time to be introspective and humane. Where the pressure is intense (either for students or professors), everybody must run to keep his seat.

The difficulty for the traditional disciplines in the humanities and social sciences (and here the natural scientists may be far ahead) is that they still behave, in large measure, as if there were nothing but Western culture, no television, no electronic circuits, no psychoanalysis, and no way of knowing about anything except through books. I'm not referring here to "teaching techniques"—which are obviously antediluvian, but to intellectual techniques, subject matter, and ways of organizing experience. What, for example, happens to our understanding of history when we can analyze not only what the man said, but the way he looked, his facial expressions, his laugh, his private off-the-cuff remarks? Will there be disciplinary techniques to handle such problems without making it necessary to become swamped by endless detail? Are there concepts to handle ambiguity or even what now seems absurd? If Hubert Humphrey is privately for a bombing halt but makes no public declarations, who is Hubert Humphrey? What is his *real* position? What is real? Do we have concepts for contradictions and ambivalence?

The mystery has suffered other blows. When the university and its scholars lost their monopoly as disseminators of news and ideas, as purveyors of information, the halo began to tarnish. What printing and the Bible did to the Church, mass media are doing to the university. The Indies? The East? Outer space? See it on television, take a plane, someone's been there. The professor tells the kids about civil liberties, search and seizure, habeas corpus. Hell, that's not the way it was in Selma, at the Pentagon, in Chicago. The cops bust in—up against the wall, motherfuckers—the sheriff is in with the KKK, the university has sold out to the Pentagon, the scholarly paper about rural development was financed by the CIA. Africa is going modern, sir; there are skyscrapers in Lagos. What do the professors know that isn't accessible to anyone who can travel, read, turn on the tube? Yes, they can deal endlessly with technical questions, or with remote matters of scholarship, but can they apply their disciplines to say something valid about the human condition? At the same time, are their ethics any higher, more noble than those of anyone else?

As the lines between the university and the rest of society became blurred, as the academy became more worldly, and as the world became more academic, the university necessarily came to be regarded as a center for technical training, social validation, and special services to government and industry. It is becoming less and less possible to distinguish professors from corporate technicians, government managers, and free-lance intellectuals. This isn't all bad, but it is new and different and confusing. Most of all, it justifies the students' demands for a voice in university government. The conservative charge, such as Barzun's, that the students don't know enough to make proper judgments is misleading because it is now apparent most professors don't know anything either. Which is to say that they don't know very much about what people should learn, should be interested in, or should be in order to have some comfort in their lives. (And, needless to say, don't know anything about teaching.) Technical questions, yes, but a man who has established his mastery as a molecular biologist is no more qualified to establish a curriculum—that is, to tell a student what he should know—than the student himself (except, of course, in the field of molecular biology).

The point is simple, but the implications are substantial. The more specialized the disciplines become, the more its practitioners become journeymen rather than doctors of philosophy. And anyone who is going to enter an apprentice relationship with a journeyman should have absolute choice about the journeyman with whom he wishes to

work. (The journeyman, if he has established his credentials in his craft, should, of course, have the full right to
determine the course of study in his field. He offers the
goods; the apprentice can accept or reject.) At the same
time, a faculty of journeymen (specialists in disciplines)
does not possess any demonstrated collective wisdom of
which the students are innocent. In a world of cultural
relativism the notion that a Ph.D in linguistics is a higher
claim to wisdom than four years with the Beatles is both
atavistic and arrogant. The medieval structure remains
(and it remains only in the university), but the Renaissance ideal that gave it justification in the academy has
vanished. A university should be a community, but in
establishing "rights," the problem of student power (or
even the distinction of "student" as against "faculty") is
clouded by the fact that in most things everybody on the
campus is an amateur.

Still, the central problem remains, and that is establishing some ground for disciplined discourse. This may be
a hopeless ideal, both for the university and for the world
of which the university is increasingly becoming an in-
distinguishable part, but it is worth trying for. Part of the
task is to stop denying the emotional, to recognize how
much of "reason" covers feelings, sensibilities, and attitudes which are not now subject to the disciplinary
arsenal. Everyone knows, as has sometimes been said, that
even college professors put on their pants one leg at a
time. Only the professors (and only some of them, at that)
still pretend otherwise. This is not to suggest that the
campus should become one huge T-group. Nonetheless,
there is a major task in developing courses of inquiry,
styles of discourse, methods of study and investigation
that cut the jungle broadside, that begin with *this* world,
and not in the undergrowth and safety of an established

field. Where the disciplines have a contribution to make, let's invite them in, but don't let them monopolize the membership list.

Robert Hutchins and Jerome Wiesner have both used the phrase "the learning society" which one can take as a prediction about the future: the university, says the crystal ball, will be disestablished. It will lose not only its repute as the prime center of intellectual and social wisdom, it will also begin to lose its grip on the accrediting and certifying functions of the larger world. As we have already noted, the mass media, and a lot of other things, are making the news available to any interested citizen, and thus "higher education," via special institutes, books, tapes, film, and travel, will not only be democratized, it will become, in a society that has solved its major production problems, a way of life. (If professors devoted less time to disseminating information, which can be disseminated a lot more efficiently in other ways, they might have more time and energy for discourse and for real questions and research. In many instances, the lecture is a sort of tribal ritual affirming the ancient, vestigial eminence of the doctor.) Management in the more affluent and modern corporations is already a kind of institutional organism for the gathering and dissemination of information: new markets and products, yes, but surely also urban and race problems, pollution, politics, and even philosophy. Government and corporate managements are going to find their way of disciplining the world—of controlling spirits. But insofar as they don't represent the individual, the human being with his particular problems, desires, wishes, fears, and hopes, some other institution must. One of the major criticisms of the university during the past decade is that it has said yes too often—yes to government, to industry, to weapons research. What it will have to do now is to reestablish some autonomous identity, and some way, therefore, of knowing when to say no. But in the process of establishing that identity, it will also have to decide just what it, as a university, can do, that someone else can't do just as well. Classical languages and medieval history by themselves aren't enough. Neither is physics. The matter is to invent new intellectual tools that can enable men to reestablish a sense of control over the universe, or at least a sense of themselves within it. Most of all, it must help reestablish belief in that most utopian of ideals: that there are still things to learn which are really worth knowing.

[1968]

About the Author

PETER SCHRAG was born in Karlsruhe, Germany, in 1931. Fleeing the Hitler regime, his family arrived, via Belgium and Spain, in the United States in 1941. Mr. Shrag was educated in the New York City school system and at Amherst College.

Since 1953 he has been a newspaper reporter, college administrator and, most recently, editor-at-large for *Saturday Review* and editor of *Change*.

Mr. Schrag is an established cultural critic and essayist, and his two books on the Boston public school system, *Voices In The Classroom* (1965) and *Village School Downtown* (1967), were among the earliest and continue to be among the best criticisms of public education. His articles have appeared in *Harper's, Commentary, The Nation, The New Republic, Commonweal, Change,* and *Saturday Review*.

Mr. Schrag is married and lives in New York. He is working on a new book for Random House, which will appear in 1972.